STORIES OF THE PROPHETS
IN THE HOLY QUR'AN

STORIES OF THE PROPHETS IN THE HOLY QUR'AN

Illustrated by Shahada Sharelle Abdul Haqq

NEW JERSEY • LONDON • FRANKFURT • CAIRO • JAKARTA

Written by Ruth Woodhall & Shahada Sharelle Abdul Haqq

Copyright © 2015 by Tughra Books & Işık Yayınları

18 17 16 15   6 7 8 9

All rights reserved. No part of this book may be reproduced or transmitted in any form or by any means, electronic or mechanical, including photocopying, recording or by any information storage and retrieval system without permission in writing from the Publisher.

Published by Tughra Books
345 Clifton Ave., Clifton,
NJ, 07011, USA
www.tughrabooks.com

Stories of the Prophets in the Holy Qur'an

Written by   Ruth Woodhall & Shahada Sharelle Abdul Haqq
Illustrations by   Shahada Sharelle Abdul Haqq

ISBN 978-1-59784-133-7

Printed by
Çağlayan A.Ş., İzmir - Turkey

CONTENTS

Introduction 7

Prophet Adam, the Father of Humankind 8

Prophet Enoch (Idris), a Prophet Raised to a High Rank 12

Prophet Noah (Nuh) and the Great Flood 13

Prophet Hud and the Storm 20

Prophet Salih and the Camel 24

Prophet Abraham (Ibrahim), the Friend of God 28

Prophet Ishmael (Ismail) and the Sacrifice 34

Prophet Lot (Lut) and the People of Sodom 38

Prophet Isaac (Ishaq), the Son Heralded by the Angels 42

Prophet Jacob (Yaqub), the Wise Father 44

Prophet Joseph (Yusuf), the Forgiving 46

Prophet Shuayb, the Orator 54

Prophet Job (Ayyub), Who Endured..57

Prophet Moses (Musa) and the Pharaoh 62

Prophet Aaron (Harun), the Eloquent..73

Prophet Dhu'l-Kifl (Ezekiel), a Prophet of Fortitude 76

Prophet David (Dawud), the Valiant..77

Prophet Solomon (Sulayman), the Gifted 81

Prophet Elijah (Ilyas), a Messenger of God...88

Prophet Elisha (Al-Yasa), a Believing Servant of God 89

Prophet Jonah (Yunus), the Repentant..90

Prophet Zachariah (Zakariyya), the Worshipper 96

Prophet John (Yahya), the Forbearing...99

Prophet Jesus (Isa), the Healer...101

Prophet Muhammad, the Seal of the Prophets 108

INTRODUCTION

God Almighty sent messengers to humanity to teach us good behavior and the purpose of our lives. The Holy Qur'an mentions the names of twenty-five Prophets, Prophet Adam being the first and Prophet Muhammad the last, peace be upon them all. Their stories are full of lessons for humankind as they are the best role models to follow. They demonstrate in the best possible way the great mercy of God for us. Despite all the difficulties they faced they stood firm in their faith, and with the utmost patience and perseverance they never gave up worship and teaching.

The length of these stories varies in the Qur'an. Some of them are very long (like the story of Prophet Joseph, peace be upon him) with many details, whereas some others are as short as a few sentences (like the story of Prophet Elijah, peace be upon him); sometimes only the names of the Prophets are mentioned (like Prophet Dhu'l-Kifl, peace be upon him). So, we have expanded especially some very short stories with additional information from the sayings of Prophet Muhammad, peace and blessings be upon him, and with narrations from other sources like *Qisas al-Anbiya* by Ibn Kathir. This is why some of the details in this book are not found in the Qur'anic text. Please also note that some of these narrations may have pre-Islamic content. Out of respect for the memories of the Prophets, they are not visually depicted in Islamic tradition, a principle we fully observed in this book.

We pray to God to accept this work only for His own sake. Our intentions are to enlighten and enrich children of all ages with the news of God's message to humankind as revealed in the Holy Qur'an. All that is good in this book is from God and any mistakes are from us.

بسم الله الرحمن الرحيم

In the Name of God, the All-Merciful, the All-Compassionate

PROPHET ADAM
The Father of Humankind

After God created the universe, the world, and all the plants and creatures in it, He told the angels that He was going to create human beings. The angels asked, "Will You make someone who will cause mischief and shed blood?" God said to them, "I know what you do not know."

God created Adam, the first man, from wet clay. He taught Adam the names of everything in creation, including the plants and animals, the sun, the moon, and the stars. Then, God showed the same things to the angels and said, "Tell Me the names of these things if you are truthful." The angels said, "Glory to You, the Most High, we have no knowledge except what you have taught us. You are the All-Knowing, the All-Wise."

God then said, "O Adam, tell them the names of all things." After Adam had told them the names, God told the angels to bow down to Adam. They all bowed down. But amongst the angels was Satan. Satan was a jinn, a being made of smokeless fire. Satan did not bow down with the angels to Adam and said, "I am better than Adam. You made me from fire. But him You made from clay." Satan showed his envy and arrogance.

Prophet Adam

God ordered Satan into Hell, but Satan asked God to give him some time away from Hell until the Day of Judgment. God granted Satan that time. Satan said that he would use his time to persuade all human beings to sin, so they would go to Hell too. He would whisper temptation and evil ideas into their hearts. He swore that few humans would prove themselves grateful to God. Only God's most faithful servants would remember Him.

God told Adam and his wife Eve to live in Paradise and eat freely of the things there. There was only one tree that he warned them not to come near. But Satan was jealous, and he whispered to Adam and Eve. He persuaded them both to forget that they should be obedient to God. He tempted them to eat from the forbidden tree, and at last they took the fruit. Suddenly, after sharing the fruit, they both felt ashamed. They gathered the leaves and branches from the Garden and tried to cover themselves. But God sees all things and they could not hide themselves or their sin from Him.

Adam and Eve were very sorry for what they had done. They begged God for His forgiveness and mercy. They remembered that they could not even live without His mercy. God forgave them and made Adam the first Prophet. Then, God sent them out of the Garden to live on earth for a time. God told them to remember that whoever follows His guidance does not need to fear, and after they die, they will return to the Garden forever.

Human beings cannot see Satan. This is one reason we must pray and call on God often. Human beings need God to continue to exist, for all the things we need in our lives, for guidance, and for protection from Satan and his helpers. Only God can make it easy for us to do good deeds, so we can return to the Garden forever.

PROPHET ENOCH (IDRIS) ﷺ
A Prophet Raised to a High Rank

Adam had many children, and they had many children. Among the people of Adam's family were many men who were Prophets. The Holy Qur'an mentions Enoch, the Prophet and servant of God. He was the great grandson of Adam's son, Seth. He was a man of truth and sincerity and God raised him to a high rank.

Prophet Enoch called his people to worship God alone. But very few of his people listened to his call. Most of them turned away.

Prophet Enoch taught the people to be just and fair. He taught them to pray and fast on certain days. He also taught them to give a portion of their wealth to the poor in order to please God.

He taught many more important things to his people and all of us today. He warned people not to envy others. He taught them that the best way to show gratitude for God's favors is to share these favors with others. He warned people not to be excessive or extravagant because they would not benefit from it in the end. He said that people can only really be happy when they have done a lot of good deeds because their good deeds will speak to their Lord for them on the Day of Judgment. He said that the real joy of life is to have wisdom. It is reported that Prophet Enoch was a tailor, so he is considered as the originator of this craft.

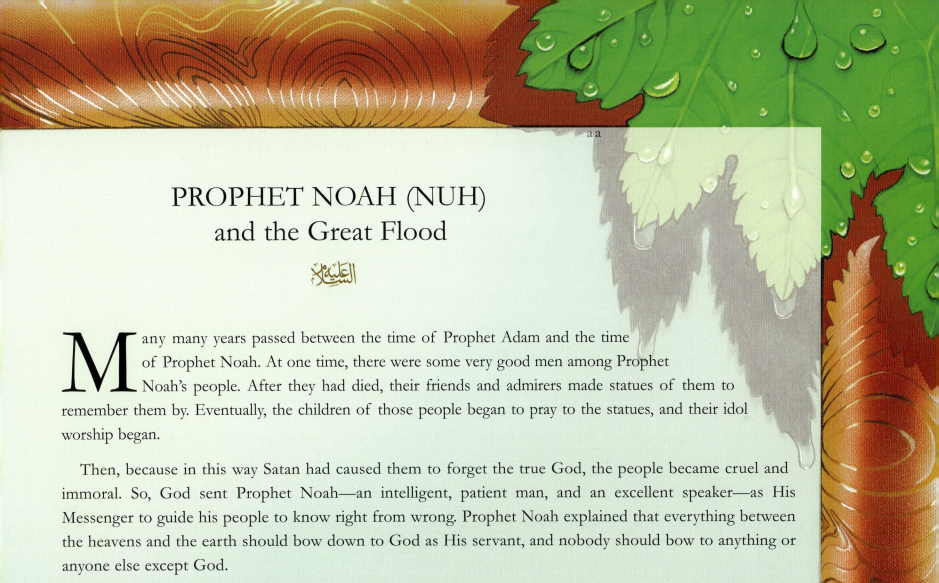

PROPHET NOAH (NUH)
and the Great Flood

السلام عليه

Many many years passed between the time of Prophet Adam and the time of Prophet Noah. At one time, there were some very good men among Prophet Noah's people. After they had died, their friends and admirers made statues of them to remember them by. Eventually, the children of those people began to pray to the statues, and their idol worship began.

Then, because in this way Satan had caused them to forget the true God, the people became cruel and immoral. So, God sent Prophet Noah—an intelligent, patient man, and an excellent speaker—as His Messenger to guide his people to know right from wrong. Prophet Noah explained that everything between the heavens and the earth should bow down to God as His servant, and nobody should bow to anything or anyone else except God.

Prophet Noah

The people listened for a while but later they called him a liar. Only the weak, the poor, and the common people believed his words. His message came as a mercy to their hearts from God.

As for the rulers, the rich, the strong, and the powerful, they told Prophet Noah, "We think you are just a man like us and nothing more." Prophet Noah promised them that he was not asking them for anything, neither wealth nor fame. For nine hundred and fifty years he went on calling his people to believe in the one God. But there were only a small number of believers. The disbelievers remained proud, arrogant, and unkind.

A day came at last when Prophet Noah prayed that the disbelievers would be destroyed:

"My Lord! Do not leave even one disbeliever on the earth. If you leave them, they will mislead your servants, the believers, and they will produce only wicked children."

God accepted this prayer. He ordered Prophet Noah to build a great ark, an enormous wooden ship.

Prophet Noah found a place outside the city and far from the sea. He collected all the wood and tools he needed and began to work. Day and night he built the ark. The disbelievers were curious and came to see what he was doing there outside the city. They laughed and mocked Prophet Noah. "Are you a madman, building a ship so far from the sea? Aren't you ashamed of yourself?" they asked. Prophet Noah replied calmly, "You will learn soon enough who will be ashamed and suffering."

Eventually, the ship was finished, and Prophet Noah patiently waited for God's command. The terrible day came when water came tumbling and foaming out of Prophet Noah's oven. This was the

Prophet Noah
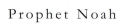

sign of the start of the great flood. He immediately rushed to open the ark and called all the believers to climb on board. Prophet Noah also took with him a male and female pair of every type of animal, bird and insect. Seeing him taking these creatures into the ark, the people laughed aloud. "What is he going to do with those animals?" they asked.

Prophet Noah's wife and his son would not join him on the ark, for they were disbelievers. When the rain started, Prophet Noah saw his son and called him on board, "O my son, come with us on the ark. Don't stay with the disbelievers." Prophet Noah's son replied, "I'll go off to a mountain. I'll be safe from the water there."

"No one can be saved from what God has commanded, except those God has mercy on," said Prophet Noah. But it was too late. The young man would not follow his father's advice, and so the son of Prophet Noah was among the people who drowned.

Prophet Noah asked the Lord why his son had not been spared. God replied that Prophet Noah's son was not of the righteous people. Then, Prophet Noah asked God to forgive him for his question, for God knows what we do not know.

Rain poured from the sky in torrents. Such rain had never been seen before. Every stream swelled, every river bank overflowed. The rivers rushed into the sea, and the sea level rose and rose. Valleys, hills and mountains, villages, towns and cities, all sank beneath the surging waters.

Then, when the earth had been washed clean of wrongdoers, God commanded the rain and the water to stop. The waters sank away, and the ark came to rest on the side of Mount Judi. Peace and calm returned to the earth. Noah released the beasts and the birds to fill the earth again. As soon as the believers had climbed down from the ark, Prophet Noah prostrated in praise and thanks to Almighty God.

Later, when the death of Noah, the Messenger of God, drew near, he warned his sons never to forget that there is no god but God. He also warned them that they should never worship any other thing except God, and that they should avoid being arrogant, but should submit themselves wholly to God.

PROPHET HUD
and the Storm

For long ages, the people of Ad lived in the hills in an area probably between Yemen and Oman. The Ad people came after Noah's people. They were big and strong, and they became famous for their construction skills. Their city had many tall buildings with high towers. But the Ad people forgot to be grateful to God. They became arrogant and boastful. They bragged about how they were richer and more powerful than all the nations in the world.

They worshipped God, but they committed the greatest sin against Him. They also worshipped other things, idols and other gods. So, God sent Prophet Hud, a man from among them to teach them the right way. Hud was patient, tolerant and noble. He reasoned with them and warned them, "What is the point in these stones that you carve with your own hands and worship? The truth is that there is no god worth worshipping except the one God. You must worship God and only God."

They asked him rudely, "O Hud, do you want to be our master? What do you want from us? Riches?" Prophet Hud replied, "I don't want anything from you! I am only asking you to believe in one God, and only one God."

The Ad people argued with Hud, "So, who is going to destroy us if we do not believe in what you tell us?"

"God," Hud replied. The disbelievers answered, "We will be saved by our gods." Hud explained to them that their idols could do nothing for them.

Years went by and the Ad people became more and more difficult and obstinate. Prophet Hud warned the Ad people again and again that God punishes disbelievers, no matter how rich, powerful, or great they may be. He said, "My Lord will make another people to replace you, and you cannot harm God."

Then, there was no rain at all for a very long time. The sun beat down and baked the earth in the fields. The wells and lakes dried up and cracked. A terrible drought was covering the land. The people came to Prophet Hud and asked, "Why do we have this drought?" Prophet Hud answered, "Because God is punishing you. If you believe in Him, He will forgive you, and rain will fall, and you will become even stronger than you are now." But foolishly, they mocked him and became even more stubborn in their unbelief. So, the drought became even harsher, the plants and even the trees were dying quickly.

One day, the people came out of their houses and saw a huge and heavy cloud in the sky. "A cloud! A cloud! It's going to rain!" they shouted. They started to rejoice and celebrate, dancing about and shouting in the streets.

All of a sudden, the air changed. It was no longer as hot and dry as an oven. It was bitter cold, freezing them all to the bone. A huge wind tore out of the sky and ripped icily at trees, plants, people, and animals. The people were shocked and rushed indoors.

But the wind grew colder, faster, and stronger day after day and night after night. In the daytime, the people huddled in their houses for shelter, but the gale kept getting stronger. Even their animals were carried away by the wind. Their homes groaned and cracked, crumbling weakly away. The storm raged furiously and killed all the Ad people and destroyed every living thing.

Only Prophet Hud and his followers were saved. They traveled to another valley and lived there in peace, worshipping God alone, their true Lord.

PROPHET SALIH
and the Camel

After the Ad people had been destroyed, the Thamud people followed them. Like the Ad people, the Thamud people were also very powerful and famous, far and wide. They too built beautiful mansions on the open plains. They carved out splendid houses in the rocky hills nearby. But like the Ad people they also stopped thanking God for all His blessings on them, and they turned away from Him. So, God, in His Mercy, sent Prophet Salih to remind them.

Prophet Salih was one of the Thamud people too. They all knew that he was wise, pure and good. Prophet Salih told them that they must worship the one God and they should never forget to thank Him.

Prophet Salih had been greatly respected by his people for his wisdom and good character even before the revelation of God came to him. The rulers among his people feared that Prophet Salih's followers would increase, although most of the people did not believe his message.

"O Salih," they said, "we know you are wise and we had great hopes for you until now. Don't try to make us give up worshipping what our fathers worshipped." But Prophet Salih could not be persuaded. He warned them that God was testing them with their power and rich lands.

Prophet Salih

Then, the leaders challenged Prophet Salih, "Give us a sign then, if you are telling the truth." They demanded a special sign. Prophet Salih prayed there and then God granted Prophet Salih a huge, beautiful she-camel as a miracle. The people gasped and wailed in astonishment.

Prophet Salih said, "Now, believe and worship the one true God. A sign has come to you from God. Let her graze on God's earth and let no harm come to her or you will be punished." God told Prophet Salih that the camel and the people must share the water in the town's oasis.

For a time, the camel grazed and drank freely. But all the while, the disbelievers were stirring trouble. They held a secret meeting, and they hatched a plot to kill the she-camel. Altogether, there were nine men in the gang.

Together, they laid an ambush. Then, the gang attacked the beautiful and defenseless camel cruelly and the poor animal died horribly.

Prophet Salih warned them, "Enjoy life for three more days, and then the punishment will come down upon you. God's promise is never broken." The disbelievers were bold and laughed at Prophet Salih. Instead of asking God for mercy, by the evening of the same day the gang had started to plan to kill Prophet Salih. They had another secret meeting. They swore to kill Prophet Salih and his family in a secret attack at night.

That night, before they could kill him, Prophet Salih left the town with his family and other believers. Before he left, he said sadly, "My people, you don't love people who give you good advice."

Then, three days after they had killed the camel, out of the clear sky, their end came upon them. Great thunderbolts crashed down upon the town, killing people, flattening all the crops and setting fire to all the bushes and trees in the fields. The earth groaned aloud, and huge quakes shook the ground, cracking the hills and mountains, so their magnificent stone houses collapsed. The people were crushed and trapped inside. All the people died and their homeland was left in ruins.

PROPHET ABRAHAM (IBRAHIM)
The Friend of God

P rophet Abraham was born into a family in Babylon. His father made his living by making wooden idols, which he sold to the idol worshippers. One day he asked his father, "What are these images that you and the people worship." His father answered, "These are our gods. Our fathers used to worship them so we worship them too." Although Abraham was very young, God had given him wisdom and understanding at an early age. So, to Abraham, the very idea that a lifeless object that cannot see or hear could be a god seemed very wrong. He said to his father, "Then, you and your fathers have been doing a great wrong."

Despite Abraham's rejection of idols and idol worshipping, one day his father asked him to sell some of the statues in the market place. Because he was obedient to his father, he took the idols to market. But he discouraged people, telling them that idols were of no use. So, he returned home without selling anything. His father shouted at him angrily, "Why are you humiliating our gods?" Abraham explained politely to his father that worshipping idols is wrong and that people should all worship the one true God. But his father was stubborn and told Abraham to leave home. Abraham's heart was full of faith, and he replied, "Peace be upon you, father. I will ask my Lord to forgive you. God has been very merciful to me."

Abraham went into the wilderness. There he asked, "My Lord, show me how you give life to the dead." God inspired Abraham with the question, "You do not believe?" "I do believe," Abraham replied, "but I am asking you to show me so that my heart will be at ease." God ordered Abraham to train four birds to come back to him, then to cut the four birds into parts, to place the parts of the birds on different hills, and then to call them. When Abraham called them, the birds returned to him quickly. Their bodies miraculously became whole again. God's power was shown to Abraham's mind and heart. He learned that when God says, "Be," then what God wants comes into existence.

God ordered Abraham to return to his people. This time he was feeling even stronger than before. When he entered the town, he was informed that the people were celebrating on the banks of the River Tigris. He was sick of their idol worship. This was an opportunity to show people their error.

The town was empty, so he went to the temple where the idol statues stood dripping with high-priced jewels, expensive clothes, and fresh, luscious foods. "What good are these gifts to idols," Abraham thought. "They can't admire their beauty, wear their bright colors, or taste the sweetness of the foods. How foolish these people are." Abraham took his hatchet and hit the idols again and again, and broke them into pieces. He left the biggest idol untouched, placed a rope through the handle of the hatchet and strung it around its neck. When the priests entered the temple, they were very upset and asked who did this to their gods. The people rushed to see the sight with horror in their hearts.

The high priest remembered Abraham had shown disrespect to the idols. So, Abraham was asked to come before the ruler of the people. Nimrod, the ruler of the people asked Abraham angrily, "Did you do this to our gods, O Abraham?" Abraham answered, "Rather, some doer must have done it." Then he diverted their attention to the big idol, "This is the biggest of them. Ask them, if they are able to speak!" Everyone looked at each other in amazement. They had realized for the first time what was obvious. Idols cannot speak or protect themselves. They are not real gods. They are only wood and stone. The high priest then said to Abraham,

disguising the erupting volcano within his heart, "You know, they cannot speak." Abraham's face brightened with this truth, and he replied, "So, should you continue to worship silent stones or will you worship God Who will answer our prayers?" Abraham appealed to the people's sense of reason, but the people did not want to accept the truth of what Abraham said. They decided to burn him alive.

Abraham was imprisoned, and everyone gathered firewood. Abraham felt safe and calm because of his faith in God. His trust in God caused him to have no fear. At the moment Abraham was thrown into the flames, the Angel Gabriel embraced him in the air and asked, "Do you need anything?" Abraham replied, "I need only God for He is nearer to me than the vein in my neck." God ordered the fire, "Be cool and peaceful for Abraham." Abraham remained calm in the middle of the fire. Not even his clothes burned. The people were shocked. When Abraham realized that his people were not going to believe in his call, he decided to emigrate. He left his people and traveled to other places.

Prophet Abraham found a group of people worshipping planets and stars. He believed it was his duty to show them the right path. He said referring to the stars, "This is my lord, is it?" But when the stars went away, he said, "I don't love things that set." When he saw the moon rising up, he said, "This is my lord, is it?" But when the moon went away, he said, "Unless my lord guides me, I shall surely be among the people in error." When he saw the sun rising, he said, "This is my lord, is it? This is greater." But when the sun went down and set, he said, "O people, I am indeed free from all that you join as partners with God.

Prophet Abraham was chosen by God to be His friend. Prophet Abraham became the father of many nations through his sons Ishmael and Isaac. Abraham called people to believe in God wherever he traveled, judging fairly between people, and guiding them to truth and righteousness.

PROPHET ISHMAEL (ISMAIL)
and the Sacrifice

When Prophet Abraham's hair had turned grey, and his wife, Sarah was already too old to have children, Sarah felt lonely in her old age without children, so she asked Abraham to take Hagar, her young servant, as his wife too. When he married Hagar, Prophet Abraham prayed to God to bless them with a son. God blessed them, and Hagar's baby was Abraham's first son. He named the child Ishmael.

After a while, God Almighty commanded Abraham to take Hagar and Ishmael to the desert and leave them there. They needed food and water, so Hagar ran rapidly back and forth between two hills to see if there was any caravan passing. Then, they saw a spring emerge miraculously under the feet of Ishmael. This spring is called Zamzam.

When Ishmael was old enough to walk by his father's side, Prophet Abraham had a dream. He learned in his dream that God was ordering him to sacrifice his own son. He loved his son very much, but he had to obey God's command. He decided to speak to his son. He said to Ishmael, "O my dear son, I have seen myself in a dream slaughtering you as a sacrifice to God. Tell me what you think about that!" Ishmael said, "Father, you must do what God commands you to do. And I will be obedient."

So, Ishmael and his father decided to obey the dream sent by God. Without telling Ishmael's mother, they set out together and walked side by side towards the place where Ishmael was to be sacrificed. On the way, Satan, disguised as an old person, tried to persuade Ishmael to disobey his father. Satan whispered that he should run away instead of being killed. But Ishmael was going to obey God and His Messenger. He quickly picked up stones and hurled them

as hard as he could at Satan, who vanished as fast as it had appeared. Satan came back to tempt Abraham and Ishmael two more times on their journey. But each time they flung sharp stones at Satan who had to run away in the end.

When they reached the place for the sacrifice, Abraham took out a blindfold for Ishmael. He did not want Ishmael to see his sadness. But Ishmael refused and told his father to blindfold himself. He said, "I am not afraid, father." Abraham put on the blindfold so that he did not have to see his firstborn son die. Then, he laid Ishmael down on his side and raised the knife high. The moment he struck down with the knife at his son's neck, God called out to him, "O Abraham! You have obeyed the dream We sent you!"

Ishmael was standing by his father alive and well. Abraham had proved his obedience, and God had sent a ram to be sacrificed instead of Ishmael. It had been a test of faith.

When Ishmael was older, he married and lived in Mecca with his wife and mother. One day, the Prophet Abraham left his wife Sarah at home and went to Mecca. There he found Ishmael sitting on the ground by the Zamzam well. He was quietly mending his arrows. Prophet Abraham greeted his son and said, "Ishmael, your Lord has ordered me to build a house for Him." Ishmael replied, "Then, father, you must obey the order of your Lord." Abraham said, "God has also ordered you to help me to do it." Ishmael, his obedient son, agreed immediately.

So, they got up and together they started building the Ka'ba. They gathered stones and Prophet Abraham set each stone carefully in place, as Prophet Ishmael handed them to him one by one. As they raised the walls, they prayed without pause, "O Lord, accept this service from us. Indeed, You are the All-Hearing, the All-Knowing." The walls became so high that Prophet Abraham could no longer stand on the ground and reach the top to set the next layer of stones in place. Then, he stood upon a large stone block to continue working on the walls. Ishmael carried on passing him the stones. As they completed each section in this way, they would move the block along and start the next section. And all the time, as they built, they kept repeating "O Lord, accept this service from us. Indeed, You are the All-Hearing, the All-Knowing." In this way Prophet Abraham and Prophet Ishmael finished building the Sacred House of God, the Ka'ba, together.

PROPHET LOT (LUT)
and the People of Sodom

Once, in the city of Sodom, there lived a people who sinned like no other people in the world before them. The evil people of Sodom used to set out in gangs to rob and kill travelers. They did all kinds of bad things in the open and without shame. The men liked to have affairs with men and not with women.

Prophet Lot lived with his family in the city of Sodom. He taught the people there about the one true God and reminded them to be grateful to Him for all their blessings. But the people's sins and crimes grew worse and worse every day. Although Lot preached and warned and taught them patiently for many years, not one man changed his behavior. They dared Prophet Lot, "If you are telling the truth, bring God's torment upon us, then." Lot could not bear their wickedness any longer. He called on God to punish the people of Sodom for their sins. God listens to His humble servants.

One day, Lot's daughter was drawing fresh water for the home at a river outside the walls of the city. She turned around to see three tall and very handsome men looking at her. They asked her for her father. She told them to wait there by the town gate until she returned. She left her water pot by the river and rushed straight to her father. "Father," she said, "there are three strangers at the town gate and they are asking for you." She added, "I'm afraid I have never seen men as handsome as these before, father." Prophet Lot had a bad feeling. He ran straight to the men who were asking for him, before anyone else could see them, and said, "Peace be on you, brothers. Have you come to visit, or are you passing through?" They answered, "We have come to carry out an important mission in this town."

Prophet Lot was very worried. "In all my life, I have never come across people as bad as those in this town. You need to beware of them," he warned. He secretly led them through the town to his house.

But the news spread quickly all around the town. Everybody was curious to see the young men. Soon after the three men had entered his home, Prophet Lot noticed a big crowd coming towards his house. The men in the crowd were demanding to come in so they could see the handsome strangers. He begged the men of the town to leave his guests in peace. He tried to persuade them do to what God has made lawful. "Understand," he shouted to them, "God commands men to marry women, and women to marry men. Be careful of your duty to your Lord."

Before Prophet Lot could answer, the rowdy mob broke down his door and crashed into the house. The angels stood firmly in front of the evil people, and the Angel Gabriel made a sign that caused the evil people to lose their vision. At this, the crowd took fright and ran away from the house into the night screaming wildly. The angels turned to Prophet Lot. They told him to gather up a few things, take his family and run away from the city immediately before dawn without looking back. If they turned and looked back, the punishment that would strike the people of the town would also strike them. Prophet Lot quickly left his home with his family as the angels had ordered.

At sunrise, there was a terrifying, ear-splitting noise, as if the air were bursting. The ground under them buckled and heaved like a wild animal, splitting the roads and buildings into small pieces and turning everything upside down. Hard hot stones rained down from the sky, striking all those who had rushed out of their homes.

In the meantime, Prophet Lot and his family continued to flee without turning round. But his wife was one of the wicked, disobedient people of the town, and like all the rest, she died then and there. Today, there is a lake where the town once existed. Its water is saltier than the seas. It is called the Dead Sea.

PROPHET ISAAC (ISHAQ)
The Son Heralded by the Angels

By the time Prophet Abraham and his wife Sarah had reached their old age, they no longer expected that Sarah would have any children. But nine years after Prophet Abraham's son Ishmael had been born to his wife Hagar, angels came to Prophet Abraham and announced that he would have a second son. This son would be born to his wife Sarah. His son would be a Prophet too, and the father of another Prophet. Prophet Abraham's wife Sarah was listening, and she laughed out loud at the news. "Oh, if only!" she said. "But how can it be?" she asked. "I am too old now. And so is my husband. It is foolish for me to expect a child of my own."

The angels said, "Are you doubting what God has decreed? May the mercy of God and His blessings be upon you." Sure enough, as God willed, Sarah gave birth to her first son, who was the second son of Abraham. They rejoiced and named their son Isaac, whose birth was heralded by the angels.

Prophet Isaac was one of the best of men. He was generous and did good deeds. Like his father and his brother, he guided people to the right way, to the worship of the one true God. Many Prophets would come from the line of Prophet Isaac, whereas, only one, but the most important Prophet, would come from the line of his brother, Prophet Ishmael.

PROPHET JACOB (YAQUB)
The Wise Father

Prophet Jacob married and had twelve sons. His second wife gave birth to two of his sons. Her first son was Joseph, a Prophet of God. Her second son was his beloved brother Benjamin. She died after Benjamin's birth. Prophet Jacob would suffer a lot because of what his other ten sons would do to Joseph and his brother Benjamin.

At the end of Prophet Jacob's life, when he was close to death, his twelve sons all drew close around his bed. Prophet Jacob reminded them, "O my sons, God has chosen the Faith for you. Then, be sure that at all times you are in obedience to God's will." He asked his sons, "What will you worship after me, or after I am dead?" They promised him, "We shall worship your God and the God of your fathers, Abraham, Ishmael, and Isaac; the one true God. Only to Him will we bow down." And they never joined any other gods with God. This pleased Prophet Jacob.

PROPHET JOSEPH (YUSUF)
The Forgiving

One day, when he was still a young boy, Joseph said to his father, Prophet Jacob, "Father, I had a dream. I saw the sun, the moon and eleven stars. And I saw them all bow down to me!" Prophet Jacob warned Joseph, "My dear son, do not tell your vision to your brothers or they may plot against you. For Satan is the sworn enemy of all humans, and he will try to make them sin if they hear of this."

Joseph and his brother Benjamin were very respectful and kind. Both boys had the same mother. Their beautiful behavior and their love of God made their father be compassionate toward them more than their older brothers. Prophet Jacob's other sons who had a different mother were jealous of Joseph, and they wanted to get rid of him. One of them said, "Let's throw him into a well, so some passing travelers will pick him up. They'll take him to a far country." So, they all agreed to go to their father and asked him to send Joseph with them to play. Unwillingly, Prophet Jacob gave permission. The smallest boy, Benjamin, stayed at home.

The next morning, the older brothers went out, taking young Joseph with them. They told him to take off his shirt, and then, suddenly they seized him and pushed him down the well. Joseph cried and shouted and begged them to help him out. His cruel brothers went away and left their younger brother there alone and afraid. They smeared fake blood over Joseph's shirt, and they went to their father, weeping. They said, "Father, we were racing with one another, and left Joseph on his own with our things, and a wolf attacked him and ate him all up. Look! Here is Joseph's shirt. We found it covered with blood, but we couldn't find Joseph!" Deep down

in his heart, Prophet Jacob knew that his sons were lying. He burst into tears, saying, "Rather, your souls have tempted you to do something evil. So I should show patience without complaint; I can only seek help from God."

Meanwhile, young Joseph waited in the well. He prayed to God, for he knew he was being tested. Then, God revealed to him that he was safe and should not fear. Prophet Joseph surrendered himself completely to the will of his Lord.

Soon, a caravan of traders arrived at the well. The water-carrier for the caravan dropped his bucket down into the well. Deep in the well, Prophet Joseph grabbed the bucket and tugged on the rope. The traders took Joseph with them to sell as a slave. They carried him off with them to Egypt, far from his beloved homeland of Canaan.

In the slave market, the chief minister of Egypt bought Joseph. He said to his wife, "Treat him well and honorably, and maybe he'll bring us much good, or we shall adopt him as a son." Prophet Joseph found himself in a rich and luxurious mansion with a kind master. As he grew up in the minister's home, the purity of his heart showed in Joseph's face, increasing his outer beauty. He became an extraordinarily handsome young man. God gave him power, knowledge, and full Prophethood.

Seeing Prophet Joseph's great beauty and good character, the minister's wife fell in love with him. One day, the woman was unable to control her feelings and asked Prophet Joseph to stay with her. Prophet Joseph was shocked. In fear of God's punishment, he raced to the door to get away from his master's wife. She chased after him and, trying to stop him leaving her, she grabbed at the back of his shirt and ripped it. At that very moment, as Joseph flung the door open, outside stood her husband and one of her relatives. Their eyes opened wide in astonishment, and they gazed at the strange scene before them.

They looked at the shirt, which was torn from the back, so it was clear evidence that the woman was guilty. The minister was angry. She was embarrassed and ashamed. The minister told his wife she must ask her servant for his forgiveness and so she did. Then, Joseph forgave her, and her husband forgave her too.

Prophet Joseph

Yet, rumors spread throughout the city. The minister's wife was very unhappy to be talked about in such a bad way, so she made a plan. She arranged a party for all her friends and ordered her maids to serve each guest a whole fruit with a knife to cut it with. Then all of a sudden, she called for Joseph to come in. As soon as they saw Joseph, all the women gasped in wonder and said, "No man is this handsome," "Perhaps he is a noble angel." And as they stared open-mouthed, without noticing what they were doing, they all cut right through the fruit and into their hands. Then, the chief minister's wife stood up and announced, "I do not deny that I tempted this man. You too have been enchanted by Joseph. If he does not do what I want, he shall be imprisoned." Prophet Joseph refused the woman again and prayed to God to be protected from the sin. So, he found himself locked up in prison.

In Prophet Joseph's third test, God blessed him with the ability to explain the meaning of dreams. One day, the king of Egypt said to his courtiers, "I had a dream. In my dream I saw seven thin cows eat seven fat cows, and seven green ears of corn, and seven others withered. Chiefs, explain to me my dream." No one around the king could interpret the dream. The cupbearer of the king who had been in prison with Joseph long ago remembered that he could explain dreams. So, he went to prison to ask Joseph.

"For seven years Egypt's farmers will harvest plenty of crops," Joseph told the cupbearer. "If the land is properly cultivated, there will be much more harvest than the people will need. What they do not use must be stored for seven years. After that, nothing will grow for seven years. During this time the stored grain can be used to feed the people." Prophet Joseph also advised that even during the famine years, they should save some grain to be used as seed the next spring. "After seven years of drought, there will be a year during which water will be plentiful. If the water is used properly, grapevines and olive trees will grow in abundance, providing plenty of grapes and olive oil," Prophet Joseph concluded.

The king was astonished and delighted. He commanded that Prophet Joseph should be set free from prison. However, Prophet Joseph refused to come to the king until he proved his innocence in the matter of the ladies who cut their hands and the minister's wife. The minister's wife admitted that she was the one who had tried to seduce Prophet Joseph.

Then, the king commanded, "You are intelligent and trustworthy. You must be one of my ministers." Prophet Joseph asked, "Your Majesty, put me in charge of Egypt's grain stores. I know how important they are and I know what to do." For seven years he made sure that the grain storehouses were filled higher and higher every harvest. When at last drought struck, the crops failed in Egypt and the lands all around, and famine followed. As well as feeding the Egyptian people from the grain stores, Joseph advised the king to sell his spare grain at a fair price to people from the neighboring countries. The king agreed and the good news spread rapidly.

Prophet Jacob sent ten of his sons, all except Benjamin, to Egypt to buy grain. When they called on the minister to buy their share of the grain, they did not recognize him as their brother. But Prophet Joseph immediately knew them. He was very welcoming and kind to them. He gave them a camel load of grain, enough for their family for a few months. Then, he said, "Next time you come, bring your younger brother and I will give you twice as much." Prophet Joseph also put their money secretly back into their bags to make sure they would come with his brother.

The brothers returned to Canaan, and before they even unloaded their camels, they rushed to their father and asked him to send Benjamin with them to Egypt next time. Remembering Joseph, Prophet Jacob refused them at first. When they unloaded the sacks, they were astonished to find the bag with the money they had paid still inside. They realized it was no mistake. Showing their money to Prophet Jacob, they tried to reason with their father again. This time they were successful. Prophet Jacob asked them to swear an oath and then gave permission for them to take Benjamin with them.

When the brothers entered Egypt, Prophet Joseph welcomed them even more warmly than before. He prepared a feast for them where he had his brother Benjamin sit next to him. Later that night, when everyone had eaten and fallen asleep, Prophet Joseph spoke secretly to Benjamin, "I am your long-lost brother! I am alive and safe. There is no need to weep anymore over what they did." God had brought them together again after all those years. But he asked Benjamin to keep it a secret just a short while longer.

The next day, while his brothers' provisions were being delivered, Prophet Joseph told his men to push the king's golden cup into the saddlebag on Benjamin's horse. Then, their bags were searched at the gate of the city, and Benjamin was arrested for stealing the cup. This was a trick Prophet Joseph played to keep Benjamin with him. Fearing that their father would never trust them again, they begged, "Please, he has a father who will cry for him. Take one of us instead, we beg you." Prophet Joseph said, "God forbid that we should be so unjust! He is the only one we can punish."

When the brothers returned home and told their father what had happened, Prophet Jacob wept so much that he lost his sight. He told them to return to Egypt and try to get Benjamin released.

They went to Egypt, and pleaded with Prophet Joseph, "O ruler of the land, have mercy on us and our poor father, who has gone blind with grief through losing his sons." Then, Prophet Joseph thought that it was time to reveal the truth. "I am Joseph," he said, and upon hearing this they began to tremble with fear. Prophet Joseph comforted them. "I forgive you here and now," he said. Prophet Joseph embraced them with love and together they wept with joy.

"Take this shirt of mine and go home," Prophet Joseph said. "Lay the shirt over my father's face. He'll get his sight back. Then, come back and bring to me all of our family." They headed back for Canaan. When they arrived home, the wife of the eldest son remarked, "Your father has come out of his room today, and all day he has been saying that he can smell Joseph. It is very strange." They placed the shirt over the face of their father, and his sight became clear again. They told him all that had happened, and they wept and said, "Father, O Father, ask forgiveness from God for our sins." Like his son, Prophet Jacob forgave them for what they had done to him.

As Prophet Joseph had requested, the entire family departed Canaan and traveled to Egypt. When they entered Egypt, Prophet Joseph took his parents into his home. He brought his family to stand before his throne in Egypt. They all bowed down before him.

Prophet Joseph said, "O Father, this is the dream I had before! My Lord has made it come true. He was indeed good to me when he took me out of prison and brought you here out of the desert life, after Satan had sown bad feelings and bad thoughts against me in my own brothers. My Lord is the most generous and kind. Truly, He is the All-Knowing, the All-Wise."

PROPHET SHUAYB
The Orator

The Midian people were Arabs whose lands stretched from Maan in present day Jordan to the Gulf of Aqaba. They had strayed from the true path and started to worship idols. They had many gods.

God sent Prophet Shuayb from among the Midian people to call them back to the right way. Prophet Shuayb was a great orator, and some people called him Jethro as well. He spoke very well, with beautiful words and expressions. People really enjoyed listening to him, and he could make people think. He said, "O my people, worship God. You have no other god but Him." He warned them of the punishment that would fall on them otherwise. Instead of thinking about what Prophet Shuayb said, the leaders of the town placed a ban on people going to him to listen to his teachings. They were afraid that his beautiful speeches were too convincing.

As well as worshipping false gods, the people of Midian did other shameful things. They demanded money to let traders pass through their area. If the traders stopped in the markets to buy and sell, the Midian traders would cheat them. Sometimes the traders wanted to buy or sell grain, or precious metals, like gold and silver. Then the Midians would secretly fix their scales in their own favor, so the traders were deceived and could not get a fair price. At other times, the Midians would sell their own goods, such as cloth and things that had been made in their town. Then, they would lie about the quality of the goods and hide their faults to fool the foreign traders.

Prophet Shuayb called on his people to stop cheating, stop taxing travelers and stop barring people from coming to him to learn. He promised that if they accepted his advice, God would bless their trading and make them even more rich and successful. He said, "Do not make mischief on the earth, if you have faith."

| 54 |

Of course, the Midians could not believe him. They were so used to lying and cheating that they thought everybody else was a liar too. So, foolishly, they trusted nobody. They said to Prophet Shuayb, "We think you are a liar like us. Go on, then. If you are telling the truth, make bits of the heavens fall down on us. We dare you." Prophet Shuayb said, "My Lord knows very well what you are doing."

The leaders threatened Prophet Shuayb, "If you and your followers don't stop all this nonsense, accept our ways and come to our religion, we'll drive you all out of our city." The leaders hated Prophet Shuayb, and they would not be patient. They threatened the townspeople to stay away from this Messenger of God and not to believe him. One day, they seized all the belongings of Prophet Shuayb and his followers and drove them out of the town. Then, Prophet Shuayb prayed to God to judge who was truthful.

Then, the weather in Midian became scorching hot. The people tried to shelter in their houses and some of them went out into the hills to try to cool down. But nothing helped. Then, a huge billowing black cloud appeared in the sky and the people hoped that it would shade them from the sun and bring refreshing rain. But, then there was a sound like thunder and the earth began to shake violently. Burning rocks flew out of the dark cloud, and everyone was gasping for breath. By the next morning they all lay dead, face down where they had fallen, in their homes.

Prophet Shuayb and the believers were outside the town, unharmed and protected by God. Prophet Shuayb looked back and said, "O my people, I gave you the message from my Lord. I gave you good advice. Should I cry or be sad about a people who refuse to believe?" For many years, the ruins stood there and reminded passers-by of the evil deeds of the Midians.

PROPHET JOB (AYYUB)
Who Endured

عليه السلام

Prophet Job lived in Harran in Syria near Damascus. God blessed him with many children, large flocks of sheep and a lot of land. He was a wealthy and generous man and was well respected by his people. All his life, he worked to please God. He taught his family and the community to worship the one true God. He helped the needy, weak and poor. He gave shelter to orphans, and he worshipped God sincerely.

This world is a testing ground. Our attitudes and behavior in the face of events determine how we pass the test; God Almighty rewards His patient servants who are sincere in faith. So Prophet Job faced a severe test of faith. He lost all his possessions and became very poor. Then his family had to separate from him, except for his wife. In addition to all this, he was afflicted with a terrible disease.

In the face of all these calamities, Prophet Job thought that everything God took away from him belonged to Him anyway. God gives to people as He pleases, and He takes away as He pleases. Prophet Job said he had no right and no wish to complain.

The disease made Prophet Job suffer greatly, but never once did he complain. He endured all the pain and suffering without losing his faith. He prayed and hoped for God's mercy. In the long years when he suffered, even close relatives stopped coming to see him. Only his kind and loving wife stayed with him.

But there was a point when she became really exhausted and unhappy. She thought of the old days when they had had such a good farm with so many animals and a lovely big house full of wonderful, lively children. She was not expecting all this to happen back then. Suddenly, the years of suffering and loss were too much for her to endure, and she burst into tears. Losing control, she said bitterly to her husband, "How long are you going to endure this test from our Lord? Why don't you call upon God to take away this suffering?"

Prophet Job said, "I have not suffered for as long as I was healthy and rich. I am grateful to my Lord. But I think your faith has become weak, my dear wife, and you are complaining about what God has given you. I swear that if I ever regain my health, I will punish you with one hundred strokes. Now, leave me. I no longer want your help. My Lord will do whatever he wants with me."

The disease got worse and when it affected his heart and tongue, he feared that he would not be able to worship properly. In his helpless state, Job turned to God, and asked for His mercy without complaining. "Lord," he prayed, "affliction has harmed me, so that I can no longer worship You as I must; and You are the Most Merciful of all those who show mercy."

God answered his call, "Strike the ground with your foot. A spring of water will appear for you to wash in, and as a cool and refreshing drink for you." Prophet Job struck the ground and fresh water sprang from it. He washed in the water and his body was healed. He became like a young man again.

His loving and faithful wife could no longer bear to be parted from him and returned to beg his forgiveness. Prophet Job welcomed her back. She embraced him and thanked God for His mercy. God then caused Prophet Job's wife to have a youthful appearance too. But her husband Job was concerned. He had sworn by God's name to punish her with

a hundred strokes if he regained his health. He knew if he did not do it, he would be guilty of breaking a promise to God. But he did not want to hurt his wife. In His wisdom and mercy, God came to the aid of His servant. God revealed to Prophet Job, "Take in your hand a bundle of thin grass, and strike your wife gently with it, and don't break your oath."

God continued to bless Prophet Job. His relatives came back to him and his people doubled in number. Truly God found Prophet Job to be patient and enduring. How excellent a servant he was.

PROPHET MOSES (MUSA)
and the Pharaoh

The pharaoh who ruled Egypt was a tyrant. He was cruel to the descendants of Jacob, the children of Israel. The people had to obey the pharaoh only, and they had to believe in the false gods he invented. Eventually, people began to worship the pharaoh himself as a god.

One night, the pharaoh had a dream. In his dream, he saw a fire which came from Jerusalem, where the children of Israel had come from. The fire burned down all the houses of the Egyptians and the Copts, but did not harm the children of Israel. The pharaoh woke up sweating and terrified. He called all his priests and magicians to the court and asked them the meaning of his dream. They said, "This means a boy will be born to one of the Israelite women, and he will destroy you and the kingdom of Egypt." So, the pharaoh commanded that from then on all boys born to the Israelites be killed.

In this terrible time, an Israelite woman gave birth to her son Moses. Before Moses, she also had another boy, Aaron. She gave birth in silence without a sound. She wept and feared terribly as to what would happen to her beloved son if anyone saw him or heard him cry. Then, God inspired her, saying, "Feed him first from your breasts, and then when you fear for him, cast him into the river and do not weep. We will bring him back to you and make him one of our messengers." So, one night she stepped down among the reeds of the River Nile and, with a prayer, put the baby in a chest and slid it carefully out onto the river.

Prophet Moses

The chest moved in the water all along the river bank, and right into the palace grounds. At last the chest bumped into a bend in the riverbank and came to rest just near the pharaoh's palace. The palace servants heard the cries coming from the box and looked inside. They were very surprised and took the baby to the pharaoh and his queen. When the queen saw him, God put love and tenderness for the lovely baby into her heart. The pharaoh's wife was very different from the pharaoh. He was an idol worshipper, but she believed in the one true God. She was sad because she had hoped to have a son but she could not have children. She begged her husband, "Let me keep the baby and let him be a son to us." The pharaoh had never seen his wife so happy and he was ashamed to show how cruel he was to her, so he agreed. "It's only one boy," he thought. "I suppose he won't do me any harm."

The queen called several nurses from the palace nursery to breastfeed the baby, but he would not take any of their breasts. The queen was worried and decided to send for more wet nurses from outside the palace.

Hearing this, Moses' mother ran to the palace. As soon as the child was put to her breast, he began to suckle happily until he fell asleep in her warm and loving arms. From that day onward, although nobody else knew it, Moses' wet nurse was his own mother. She continued to breastfeed him for two years. When he was bigger and no longer took breast milk, she would still come to the palace every day to visit him and care for him. Moses lived in the palace as a prince.

Years passed and Prophet Moses grew to his full health and strength and became a perfect man. God gave him Prophethood and knowledge of the true religion. He lived in the pharaoh's palace, but he knew that he believed in one God and that he was an Israelite. Because of his wisdom and goodness, people would always turn to him when they needed protection and justice. One day he was walking through the city, when he saw two men fighting. An Egyptian was beating an Israelite slave. The Israelite saw Moses passing by and begged him for help. Moses hit the Egyptian, and he died on the spot. Seeing that he had killed a human being without meaning to, Moses' heart was filled with sorrow. "O Lord, I have sinned. Forgive me!" he begged.

The very next day, he saw the same Israelite in another fight with an Egyptian. Moses was angry now. "You! You are always fighting and causing trouble!" he said. "You start a new fight every day." The Israelite was afraid, but he argued back. He shouted loudly at Moses, "So, what are you going to do about it? Are you going to kill me like you killed that poor guy yesterday?" This shocked the Egyptian man that the Israelite had been fighting with. He quickly ran and reported Moses to the authorities. A short time later, as Moses was continuing on his way quietly through the city, a friend from the other side of the city came running. He found Moses and warned him urgently, "Moses, I've heard that the chiefs have decided to take action against you. They are going to put you on trial. It's the death penalty for killing an Egyptian. You need to get out of Egypt as fast as you can."

Prophet Moses left in a hurry with no spare clothes and only sandals on his feet. He walked through the desert towards Midian, the nearest place where people lived between Syria and Egypt He walked for eight nights. At last he came to the waterhole outside Midian. He saw a group of shepherds with their sheep drinking at the waterhole. A short distance away he saw two young women, also with a flock of sheep. Moses said, "Let me water the flock for you." After he had watered their sheep, the sisters took their flock home and Moses stayed in the shade of the trees by the waterhole. He was alone and he prayed, "My Lord! I am weak and I need any blessing you may give me!"

He saw one of the girls had come back and was standing shyly nearby waiting for him to finish his prayers. He greeted her and she said, "My father is inviting you to our home so that he can thank you for helping us." Moses went to her father's home with her, where he was made welcome. He told the old man what had happened to him in Egypt. The old man said, "Don't be afraid. It is good that you have escaped from those wrongdoers there."

One of the girls suggested to her father that Moses could work for him as a shepherd because he was strong and had a good character. Her father asked her how she could judge his character so quickly. She answered, "When I told him to follow me to our home, he asked me to walk behind him so he could not see my shape as I walked in front." The old man was very pleased. He said to Moses, "If you will promise to work for me honestly for eight years, I would like you to marry one of my daughters." Moses agreed willingly. He married the old man's daughter and looked after the sheep for ten years.

After he had completed those ten years, Moses and his family left Midian. He wanted to go to Egypt, so they traveled through the desert. They passed Mount Sinai and just after nightfall, they came to the valley of Tuwa. In the darkness Moses saw a fire burning in the distance. "I'll go and fetch a burning branch and set a fire here so we'll stay warm tonight," he told his wife.

As he approached the fire, he heard a powerful voice, "O Moses, I am God, the Lord of the Universe. Throw your staff down on the ground," commanded God. Prophet Moses cast his staff down on the ground and to his amazement, it became a snake.

"Don't be afraid. Grasp it and pick it up. We shall return it to its former state. Now, press your right hand to your left side. It will come forth white and shining without stain," said God.

Prophet Moses obeyed and everything happened as God said. Then, God spoke to Prophet Moses again, "You have been given two signs by your Lord. Now go to Pharaoh and his chiefs, for they are an evil gang and have broken all my laws." Moses was afraid he would be arrested and said, "My Lord, I killed a man there and I'm afraid they may execute me for it." God promised that he would be safe and put Moses' heart at ease. Then, Moses prayed, "O Lord, make my task easy for me. Loosen any knot from my tongue so that I may convince them of the truth. Give me a helper from my family, Aaron, my brother. Add to my strength through him and make him share my task, so that we may celebrate

Your praise." God said, "It is granted to you. Keep Me in your remembrance. Now go to Pharaoh and speak mildly to him. Perhaps he might fear Me. Tell Pharaoh to let the children of Israel go free."

Moses and Aaron went to Pharaoh and delivered their message. Moses spoke to him about God, His mercy and worship. Pharaoh listened to Moses but he had no respect for him. He asked, "What do you want from me?" Moses answered, "Release my people, the children of Israel from slavery. Allow them to leave Egypt with us." Pharaoh asked, "Why would I let my slaves go?" Moses replied, "They are the slaves of God, Lord of the Worlds."

At this, Pharaoh became irritated. He reminded Moses of the generosity and care he and his wife had shown to Moses when he was a baby. Then, he began to threaten him. "If you worship any god other than me, I will put you in prison," he said. Prophet Moses refused. "What if I give you a sign?" "A sign?" said the pharaoh. "Oh sure, give me a sign if you can, Moses." First, Prophet Moses threw his stick on the ground in front of the throne, and it turned into a huge snake, coiling and writhing. Then, he slid his right hand into his robe under his left arm. When he pulled it out, his hand was shining brilliantly.

Pharaoh was afraid that he would lose his power if people believed in Moses' message after what they had seen. "Have you come back here to drive us out of our land with your magic, Moses?" he asked. "Well, we'll see about that. There's a festival coming up. We'll have a competition between my magicians and you. It will be in a public place. That way everyone will be equal with no cheating and it will be fair. Our Egyptian magic is better than anything you can show us." Moses agreed: "Fine. Your festival day can be the day of the competition. Let everyone be there when the sun is high so there are no tricks in the darkness."

Pharaoh called a meeting with his ministers and advisers. Behind closed doors, they discussed what they were going to do. The Egyptian magicians planned and invented new tricks and practiced them again and again in preparation for the competition.

The day of the competition came. Before it started, Moses said to them all, "You have been warned! If you lie against God, He will destroy you completely. You cannot win against God." They did not answer, but asked, "Do you want to go first or shall we?" Moses said, "No, you go first." They threw down a rope and some sticks, and they looked as if they were moving across the floor by themselves. Then, Moses threw down his staff from his right hand. Once again, it became a huge coiling snake, and it swallowed up the rope and all the sticks thrown by the pharaoh's magicians.

The magicians all fell on their faces. They said, "We believe in the Lord of Aaron and Moses." Pharaoh was filled with fury and panic. He was going to lose his kingdom and his power. "How dare you believe in him before I give you permission? I'll have your hands and feet cut off on opposite sides! I'll have you crucified on the trunks of palm-trees!" But his threats did not move the magicians. They knew that their tricks were fake and that what Moses had shown them was real. It was a sign from God, and they believed. After the competition, Pharaoh had the magicians executed horribly to frighten the public, but he had already lost face, and he started to lose influence in his court and even in his family.

He called another council of ministers to decide what to do. Pharaoh said, "Let me have Moses killed. Then, we'll show the people that calling on his Lord won't save him! Otherwise, he might persuade the people to change their religion, or cause trouble all over my kingdom!" Then, a member of Pharaoh's family, a man who was hiding his faith in God, said, "It's not a good idea to kill a man because he says, 'There is one God.' He gave you clear signs that no one can explain away, didn't he? O my people, I am afraid that something terrible may happen to us, as it happened to the people of Noah, and Hud, and Shuayb, and others too." The man made the council doubt the pharaoh's wishes and so they did not agree to have Moses executed.

Prophet Moses

While the believing Egyptian man argued in the council, there was an Israelite called Korah in the town who had become a friend of the Egyptian disbelievers. He had become extremely rich, but he refused to give the money he should have given in charity every year. He would go about town in fancy clothes and spend his money extravagantly in front of other people. Moses went to see him and reminded him that all his blessings came from God. He reminded him of his duty to the poor, to widows and orphans and travelers. "Pah!" he said. "Blessings? Duty? I am rich because I am smarter than the rest of you! I did it all myself! I'm a self-made man!" Moses went away without another word. A few days later, the ground collapsed under Korah's house. It sank into an underground pit, crushing all the rich furnishings, luxuries and treasures that Korah was so proud of. Inside the house perished the arrogant Korah.

Prophet Moses and Prophet Aaron went back to Pharaoh's court and warned him that they would be punished for making Israelites slaves. Then, several calamities came upon the Egyptians one after another. First, the River Nile did not flood the plain and soak the dry land; then it swelled and crashed over everything. Later, God sent locusts to Egypt to consume all the crops, and then vermin to bite and give the Egyptians diseases, and then frogs to spread everywhere and to spoil their lives, and finally the Nile water changed into blood. At each of these calamities, the Egyptians went to Moses and promised to release the Israelites. He prayed to his Lord, and they were saved, but the Egyptians broke their promise.

Then, God told Prophet Moses to leave Egypt with his people at nightfall and to go secretly towards the sea. By morning, Pharaoh had heard that the Israelites were leaving, and he ordered his soldiers to march quickly and trap the Israelites at the seashore. The Israelites were terrified to see the wide body of water in front of them and the great army of Pharaoh advancing behind them. Then, Almighty God revealed to Prophet Moses to fear only Him, and to strike the water with his staff. Suddenly, the sea rolled back and a dry path appeared between the waves for the Israelites to cross the sea.

Praising God and trusting in Him, the Israelites walked through the path in the sea to the other side. The Egyptian army obeyed the pharaoh's orders and began to chase the Israelites to the other side of the sea. Almighty God caused the sea to roll back over their heads. The wet sand sucked at the soldiers' feet. Then, their heavy uniforms, their chariots and weapons held them down as the swirling waves advanced on them. Not one could swim away. Every last one of them drowned.

As the sea dragged Pharaoh down, he cried out, "I believe that there is no god except Him Whom the children of Israel believe in." But it was too late. God said, "But a little while before, you were in rebellion against Me. And you did mischief and violence. Only your body shall be saved, so that you may be a sign to those who come after you."

Prophet Moses and the Israelites were free. Now, they faced another test. They traveled through the Sinai Desert in search of a new land where they could settle and live in peace. When they were hungry, God sent flocks of small birds called quail to them, and each bird carried a fruit called manna. When they were thirsty, God inspired Prophet Moses to strike a rock with his staff, and suddenly twelve springs of fresh water came from the rock for Moses and the Israelites to drink. Prophet Moses then went to Mount Sinai and spent forty days in worship. At the end of forty days, he received the revelation. Before he went he placed his brother Prophet Aaron in charge of the Israelites. "While I am away, take my place and act in the right way by ordering the people to obey God and to worship God alone," said Prophet Moses.

PROPHET AARON (HARUN)
The Eloquent

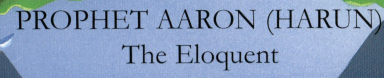

Aaron was Moses' brother. When God told Moses that he was to be a Prophet, Moses asked, "And my brother Aaron—he is more eloquent than I am and can persuade the pharaoh and the people—so send him with me as a helper, to confirm and strengthen me. For, I fear that they will accuse me of lying." So, Aaron was appointed by God to help his brother Moses to free the children of Israel from the Egyptians.

While they were crossing the desert, God commanded Prophet Moses to worship for thirty days and nights and then made it up to forty by adding ten more days and nights. Prophet Moses left his people at the foot of the mountain and went to stay on the mountain alone. He said to his brother, Prophet Aaron, "Take my place among my people, lead them in the right way of obeying and worshipping God alone. Do not let the troublemakers among them lead you all astray. Keep them united."

Prophet Aaron was responsible for leading the worship of the people. However, when he was alone without his brother, the idol worshippers among the Israelites immediately took advantage. They collected all their gold together, melted it down and made an idol in the shape of a cow. They made the idol in such a way that when the wind blew on it, a noise like the noise of a real cow came from the statue. For several dark nights, the people listened to this sound and worshipped the idol. The idol worshippers' leader was Samiri. Prophet Aaron warned them, "This thing is no more than a statue. Only God is God and only He is worthy of worship, and Moses is His Messenger." But they would not listen. Samiri argued with Prophet Aaron, "We will not stop praying to it until Moses returns to us. Where is Moses now if he is our leader?"

Not all of the Israelites worshipped the golden cow, so they started to split into two groups. Prophet Aaron warned them again and again. Eventually, Samiri threatened to kill him. Prophet Aaron and the believers thought about fighting against Samiri and his followers, but Prophet Aaron believed that fighting was not the best way to get the people to believe in the truth. Patiently, he continued to try to persuade them.

While he was on the mountain, Prophet Moses had received revelation from God. When he came down the mountain back to his people, he was furious to see what was going on. He shouted, "What an evil thing you have done while I was away. Are you trying to be destroyed by your Lord?" He put down the stone tablets where God's orders were written, grabbed his brother by the hair of his head, and dragged him to him. Prophet Aaron said, "Brother! I tried to stop them but they wouldn't listen to me! They were going to kill me! They'll be happy to see you beat me. Don't make them happy. Don't blame me as you blame them. I didn't do wrong. I didn't fight them in case the people split into two groups. You told me to keep them all together."

Prophet Moses' heart softened, and he called on God to forgive him and his brother. Those who worshipped the calf were punished in this life, and they will also be punished in the hereafter. Those who truly ask God for forgiveness will be the only exception. For, God is the Most Forgiving, the Most Merciful. Prophet Moses picked up the stone tablets again. In them there was guidance and mercy for those who fear their Lord.

PROPHET DHU'L-KIFL
A Prophet of Fortitude

"Dhu'l-Kifl" is not the name of this blessed Prophet; it is a title which means "a man of great portion." This title is given to him because of his exalted personality and lofty degree in the Hereafter. He was among the children of Israel. He was a Prophet of fortitude and patience.

PROPHET DAVID (DAWUD)
The Valiant

Prophet David was an Israelite. His story begins at a time when the disbelievers drove the people of Israel out of their land. The believers armed themselves against the disbelievers and prepared to go to war to win back their land.

The leader of the disbelievers' army was a huge soldier named Goliath. When the two armies lined up facing each other, Goliath called out a challenge to single combat to any soldier from the believers' army. This was the custom in those days. Goliath's reputation and his strength were so great that the Israelites did not have the courage to volunteer. The king of the believers offered his beautiful daughter in marriage to the man who would fight Goliath, but even this offer did not bring a break in the deadly silence among his soldiers.

Then, to everyone's surprise, a slim, young man stepped forward from behind the ranks. He was dressed like a shepherd, and that was his work. The enemy soldiers roared with laughter. The young man was David. The king was surprised by young David's bravery and trust in God. David picked a few sharp pebbles off the stony ground. He pushed them into a leather pouch. He hung the pouch over his shoulder next to his slingshot. He was ready.

David walked out into the space between the two armies where Goliath was waiting. He prayed, "O God, please protect me from this gigantic man and grant me victory!"

Prophet David

Goliath looked down from his great height on the slim young man and laughed out loud. "I will cut off your head with one small swipe of my sword!" he roared. David slipped his slingshot off his shoulder and quickly placed in it a pebble from his pouch. He swung it round his head until it made a whooping noise, and aimed at Goliath. He flicked his wrist deftly, and the pebble shot from the whirling sling with the speed of an arrow and hit Goliath's forehead with great force. His head cracked, blood gushed, and Goliath slumped to the ground before he had even unsheathed his sword. When the disbelievers' army saw their splendid general lying lifeless in the dirt, they scattered in disarray. The Israelites triumphed in the battle and regained their glory and honor that had been lost for a long time.

Now, the young David was a hero to the Israelites. The king kept his word and gave his daughter to the young warrior as his wife. Prophet David became one of the king's chief advisors. However, David was not deceived by his fame and success. Instead, he went out of the city to stay in the desert for some time, glorifying God.

God had chosen David to be a Prophet and revealed the Psalms to him. David recited his scripture while the mountains joined his praise and the birds gathered and glorified God all around him. The plants, birds, beasts, and even the mountains responded to his voice. This was a miracle from God. It was not the only miracle God granted to Prophet David, for God also gave him the gift of understanding the languages of birds and animals. Prophet David fasted every other day and got up in the night for worship since he wished to be a truly thankful servant to God.

His people had to fight many wars, and they found that their iron armor was too solid and heavy to let them move and fight as they needed. David thought and prayed about this problem. One day he was holding a piece of iron. He realized in surprise that God had made it flexible for him and he was able to shape it easily. He prostrated himself in gratitude. So, he was able to show the metalworkers how to make armor out of metal chain links and solve the problem for his soldiers.

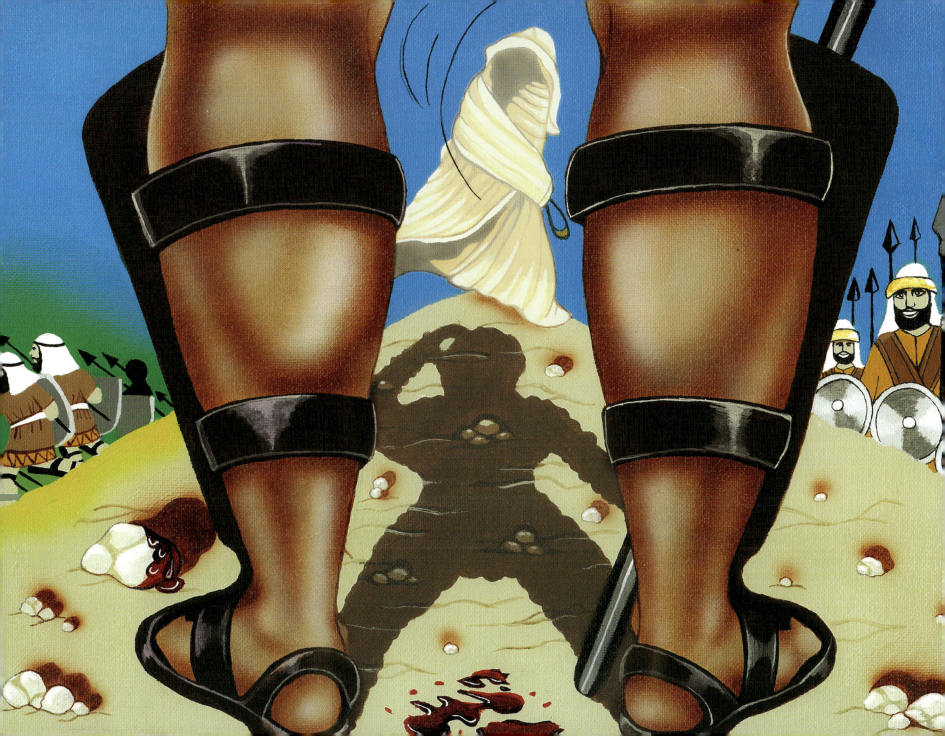

Prophet David

God granted Prophet David great influence. The people praised and loved him. After the king died, Prophet David was chosen by the people to be king. His kingdom was strong and great, and his enemies feared him and did not dare to go to war against him. He was a just and righteous ruler, He brought peace and prosperity to his people, and God honored him as a messenger. He had a beautiful voice and he delivered God's message to the people through this precious gift of his. When he recited the Psalms, it was as if the rest of creation chanted with him. People listened as if in a trance.

Prophet David was a king, but he made and sold weapons to make his living, instead of taking anything from his people. He divided his day into four quarters: one to earn a living and to rest, one to pray, one to listen to his people's complaints and requests, and the last one to teach. He had helpers to listen to his people's problems too so they were never neglected.

One day, David was praying in his prayer niche. His guards did not usually let anyone interrupt him, but that day two men managed to enter his room. "Who are you?" he asked. One said, "We have not come to hurt you. We have an argument we want you to settle for us." Prophet David said, "What is the argument about?" The first man said, "My brother here has ninety-nine sheep, and I have only one. It's true he gave it to me, but now he has taken it back without asking me." David, without asking the man's brother to explain, answered, "He did you wrong by taking the sheep back. Indeed, many partners are unfair to each other, except for those who are believers." The two men disappeared instantly. Prophet David understood that they had been two angels sent to test him. This knowledgable Prophet suddenly realized that it is unwise to make a judgment without listening to both sides of the story. Prophet David worshipped God, glorified Him and sang His praise until he died.

PROPHET SOLOMON (SULAYMAN)
The Gifted

Prophet Solomon was the son of Prophet David. As a child, he spoke intelligently and acted with such wisdom that it was clear that he would one day be a very capable leader. One day two men came to Prophet Solomon. One of them said, "O Prophet! I have a field and this man's sheep got into my field at night and ate up all the grapes I was growing. I have come to ask for compensation." Solomon, who was there with his father, spoke up, "The owner of the sheep should take care of the field until new grapes grow. The owner of the field should take the sheep and make use of their wool and milk until his field has recovered. If the grapes grow, and the field and the grapevines recover, then the field owner should take his field and give back the sheep to their owner. Otherwise, he should keep the sheep." Prophet David was pleased. "That is a sound judgment. Praise be to God for granting you wisdom."

Another day two women brought a baby boy to Prophet David. A wolf had eaten the son of one of the women, and each one claimed that the boy that was left—the one they now brought before the king—was hers. Prophet David listened to them both and then decided to give the boy to the older woman. This was because she seemed to present strong evidence that it was her child, and it was the custom of the land in doubtful cases to give the child to the older woman. Then, Prophet David asked his son's opinion. Prophet Solomon said to the court, "Bring me a large, sharp knife and I will cut the boy in two and divide him between the women, for this is fairer." The younger woman cried, "Oh no! Don't kill him. Give my boy to her! But please don't kill him!" Then, Prophet Solomon said to the older woman,

"May God have mercy on you for your sad loss of your son and for lying. He is the younger woman's son, so give him to her."

After his father's death, Prophet Solomon became king. He asked God for a kingdom like none that any king after him would have, and God answered his prayer. As well as giving him wisdom, God blessed Solomon with many other gifts. Prophet Solomon could command the winds and travel on them. God taught him the language of the birds. He enslaved the jinn (unseen beings made of smokeless fire) so they had to work for him, diving for pearls, building and sculpting metal and stone. God inspired Solomon to teach men and jinn how to mine for metals and smelt them to make tools and weapons.

Once, in the afternoon, some high-bred horses were brought before him for his inspection. After watching and admiring them for some time, he said, "My love for these horses is not for themselves, but because they serve to remind us of the beauty and generosity of my Lord." Then, he rubbed down their legs and their necks himself.

One day he assembled an army of jinn, human beings, and birds and led them out on maneuvers under his command. They marched until they reached a valley of ants, when Prophet Solomon heard one of the ants call to the others, "Ants! Get into your nests, or King Solomon and his army might crush you by accident." King Solomon smiled at her trust in him and said, "My Lord! Inspire and guide me so that I may thank You for Your blessings which You have granted me and my parents."

There was a special bird, called the Hoopoe bird, that Prophet Solomon would call to look for water in the desert whenever the army needed it. One day as Prophet Solomon was inspecting the birds of his army,

he noticed that the Hoopoe was missing. Prophet Solomon said, "How is it I don't see the Hoopoe? Is he absent?" It was not long before the Hoopoe arrived.

He announced, "I have obtained some important information, and I have flown to you all the way from Sheba. I found a woman there. She is ruling over the people, and she has a great throne. But I found her and her people prostrating to the sun instead of God. So, they have no guidance." He told them that the queen of Sheba's name was Balqis. Her land extended over Yemen and part of Abyssinia. Prophet Solomon said, "We will see whether you are telling the truth." He wrote a letter to Queen Balqis and ordered the Hoopoe to deliver it to her.

The Hoopoe bird dropped the letter in the court of the queen before her throne. Balqis picked it up and read it. She immediately gathered her council of chiefs. She said, "O chiefs, see, an honorable letter has been brought to me. It is from Solomon, and it reads, 'In the Name of God, the All-Merciful, the All-Compassionate. Do not defy me, but come to me in submission.' O chiefs, what do you advise? You know that I never make a decision on a matter unless you are with me." They said, "We have great power, and we have great courage, but this decision is yours." Queen Balqis said, "When kings invade a country, they cause destruction and corruption in it, and bring down its nobles. So, for now I will send a present and see what answer my envoys bring back."

So, Queen Balqis, intending to avoid a war against King Solomon, sent him a lavish gift of precious stones and jewels. The ambassadors of the queen presented the gifts to Prophet Solomon and offered the queen's respect. Prophet Solomon told them, "God has given me great wealth, a vast kingdom, and Prophethood. I do not need your gifts. My only objective is to spread the belief in the oneness of God." He directed the queen's messengers to take back the gifts and tell their queen that if she did not stop her sun worship, he would invade her kingdom.

Upon hearing what had happened, instead of becoming angry, Queen Balqis decided to visit Prophet Solomon in his palace in Jerusalem. In the company of her royal officials and servants, the queen set off in a procession from Sheba. She sent a messenger ahead of her to inform Prophet Solomon that she was on her way.

Hearing this, Solomon said to his council, "O chiefs, which one of you can bring me her throne before they come to me in submission?" One strong and cunning jinn answered, "I can bring it to you before you rise from your council. I have the strength and skill to do it and I am trustworthy." Another one, who had some knowledge of the Book, said, "I can bring it to you even faster than he can. I can bring it in the twinkling of your eye." When Solomon saw the throne set in his presence, he said, "This wonder is out of the pure grace of my Lord so that He may test me whether I give thanks or act with ingratitude. Now, disguise her throne, and let us see whether she is able to recognize it and see what this means or whether she is among those who are not guided and refuse to believe."

When the queen arrived, they showed her the disguised throne and asked her, "Is your throne like this one?" She looked at it again and again. How could it be here before her? It was not quite the same, was it? She wrinkled her brow. It was impossible, wasn't it? But she was forced to believe her eyes. At last she said, "It looks as if this is it." She added humbly, "Before we even came here and saw this miracle, we had already decided to submit and believe in the one God." She had only been kept back from the straight path because she had belonged to a disbelieving people.

Then, Balqis was welcomed to King Solomon's magnificent palace as an honored guest. At the entrance, she saw what seemed to be a pool of clear water. She tucked her robes up above her ankles and bared her calves so that her hem would not get wet. King Solomon looked away and said,

"The palace is paved with crystal." Realizing her weakness and ignorance in comparison to King Solomon, who had the manners of a Prophet of God, she covered her legs and said, "My Lord, surely I have wronged myself by worshipping false gods. But now I submit myself, in Solomon's company, to God, the Lord of the worlds."

On a huge rock in Jerusalem, Prophet Solomon had his servants and jinn slaves build a beautiful temple to draw people to worship God. The jinn had to work in chains as a punishment for their sin of making people believe that they were powerful and that they knew the unseen and could foresee the future. As he was a Prophet, it was the duty of Prophet Solomon to remove such false beliefs from his followers.

Before Prophet Solomon passed away he asked God to make the jinn unaware of his death so that they would keep working. Prophet Solomon's body sat leaning on his staff for a year while the jinn worked day and night and a termite gnawed away at his staff from the inside. When the staff collapsed into dust and Prophet Solomon finally fell down, the jinn saw plainly that he was no longer alive. If they had known the unseen, they would not have continued to work.

PROPHET ELIJAH (ILYAS)
A Messenger of God

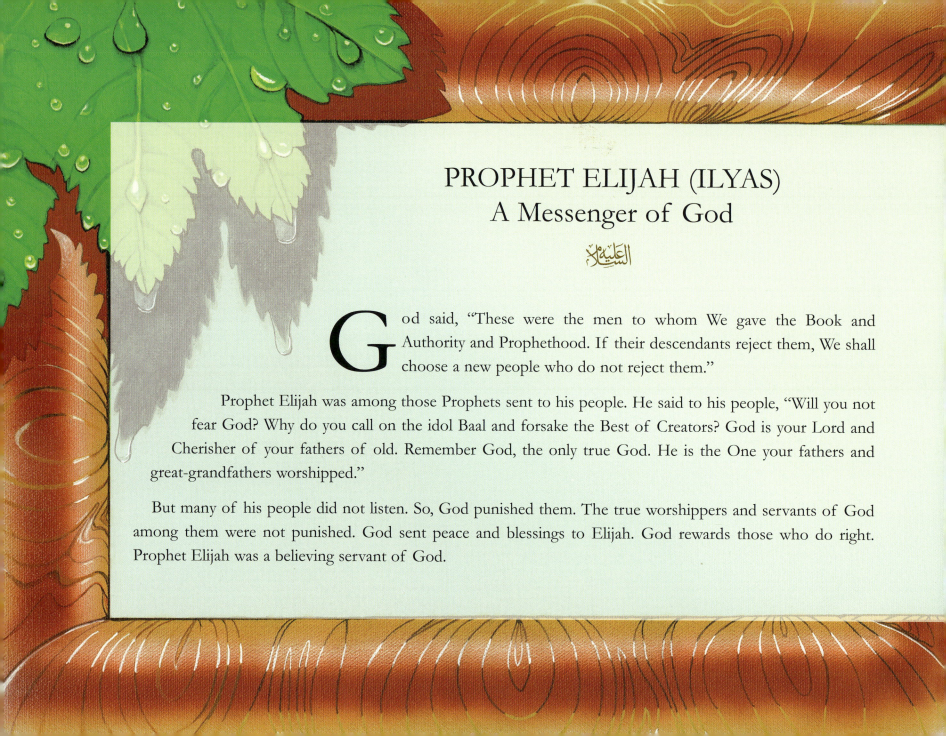

God said, "These were the men to whom We gave the Book and Authority and Prophethood. If their descendants reject them, We shall choose a new people who do not reject them."

Prophet Elijah was among those Prophets sent to his people. He said to his people, "Will you not fear God? Why do you call on the idol Baal and forsake the Best of Creators? God is your Lord and Cherisher of your fathers of old. Remember God, the only true God. He is the One your fathers and great-grandfathers worshipped."

But many of his people did not listen. So, God punished them. The true worshippers and servants of God among them were not punished. God sent peace and blessings to Elijah. God rewards those who do right. Prophet Elijah was a believing servant of God.

PROPHET ELISHA (AL-YASA)
A Believing Servant of God

Prophet Elisha was also a Prophet of God. God gave all His Prophets the favor of being honored by the nations of the earth. God chose their fathers and descendants to be guided to the straight way. Thus does God reward those who do good deeds.

PROPHET JONAH (YUNUS)
The Repentant

The people of the town of Nineveh in the Assyrian Empire worshipped idols and were proud of the many serious sins they committed. God sent Prophet Jonah to teach them to worship the one true God. But the people argued back, "In this country we have worshipped these gods for generations. We have been worshipping like this for centuries and no harm has come to us yet." Prophet Jonah spoke to them of God's blessings on them. He explained God's laws. Not one of them paid any attention to his teachings, and they all carried on their foolish and sinful customs. He warned them that God would punish them. But they were confident in their stupidity. "Come on," they said to Prophet Jonah. "We're waiting. Let it happen then." Jonah became discouraged. He left Nineveh, feeling that God's anger was about to strike down Nineveh and all its inhabitants, like the people of Noah and Hud and so many others before them.

Prophet Jonah was barely beyond the city walls, when the sky began to change color. It lit up in fierce orange, red and yellow flashing and flickering lights. It looked as if the heavens were on fire. The people's hearts filled with terror. They began to wail, "Oh, we're going to die like the people of Ad and Thamud, like the people of Noah! What shall we do?" If God was angry with them, what could protect them? All of a sudden Prophet Jonah's teaching came back to them. Of course, they had to repent and turn to God! The people all gathered together on the side of the mountain next to the town. They prayed and begged God for His forgiveness. They repented for all the sins that they had committed. Then they repented for being proud of their sins too. The mountains echoed with

their cries for mercy. Then, God forgave them. The firestorm came to an end, and all the people and the town were saved. They thanked God for His mercy and His many blessings on them. Then, they prayed for the return of Prophet Jonah. They went back to their homes and went peacefully about their business. They worshipped God as Jonah had taught and they avoided sin and followed God's law as he had commanded them.

In the meantime, Prophet Jonah boarded a small ship which had many other passengers too. All day the small ship sailed in calm waters with a good wind blowing at the sails and the bright sun overhead. However, when night fell, the mood of the sea changed. A huge storm blew up. The waves were wild, thrashing at the boat, and the wind tore and whipped at the sails. The waves rose like steep, black cliffs. They carried the ship high and threw it down into the deep dark valleys between the waves. The deck was awash and the ship was taking on water. It was close to sinking. All the while, a large whale followed, splitting the water, its huge jaws gaping wide, hungrily. God had commanded one of the greatest whales of the oceans to surface behind the ship.

Growing more desperate, the captain asked the crew to lighten the ship's load so it could float higher in the water. They threw all their cargo overboard, but still the ship was taking on water. The crew decided among themselves to lighten their load by removing at least one passenger. The captain ordered, "Make lots with all the travelers' names. The one whose name is drawn will be thrown into the sea." Prophet Jonah knew this was one of the seamen's traditions when facing a violent storm. They would sacrifice someone to the sea. It was one of the forms of idol worship at that time.

There was no escape from the lot. The sailors wrote all the passengers' names and added Prophet Jonah's name. The first name to be drawn was Prophet Jonah's. Since they knew he was the most honorable among them, they did not wish to throw him into the angry sea. So, they drew again. Again his name was drawn. They drew a third lot. Prophet Jonah's name came up again. Jonah realized that God's hand was in this, for he had abandoned his mission without God's order.

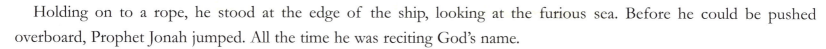

Prophet Jonah

Holding on to a rope, he stood at the edge of the ship, looking at the furious sea. Before he could be pushed overboard, Prophet Jonah jumped. All the time he was reciting God's name.

In the water, the whale swallowed Prophet Jonah into its gaping mouth and down into its great belly. Then, its belly full, the whale dived into the cold black depths of the ocean. Prophet Jonah realized that he was still alive. He was imprisoned in three layers of darkness, the darkness of the night, the depths of the sea and the belly of the whale. He felt hope and he glorified God, saying, "Glory to You. There is no God but You. Truly, I have been a sinner." He continued praying and repeating these words where he lay trapped in the belly of the whale. All the sea creatures gathered around the whale and began to celebrate the praises of God, each in its own way and in its own language. The whale also sang the praises of God and understood that it had swallowed a Prophet.

Almighty God saw Prophet Jonah's repentance and heard his prayers and glorifications in the stomach of the whale. God commanded the whale to come to the surface of the ocean. The whale obeyed. God commanded it to rise and to turn Jonah out of its belly onto the shore of an island.

Prophet Jonah found himself on the seashore. The skin all over his body was red raw from the acids inside the whale's stomach. Patiently, he endured the pain and sickness and continued to praise and thank God. God made a gourd vine grow and spread its leaves over him to protect him from the sun. Then, God made Prophet Jonah recover and forgave him.

He set out again and found his way home to Nineveh. The whole population of the town celebrated his return. They had understood God's signs, so they had rejected their idols and turned to believe in God. Prophet Jonah led a prayer of thanksgiving to their Merciful Lord.

PROPHET ZACHARIAH (ZAKARIYYA)
The Worshipper

Prophet Zachariah was a man of God in the splendid temple which Prophet Solomon had built in Jerusalem many centuries before. Prophet Zachariah served in the temple until he was a very old man. Every day he led the prayers and taught people about their religion.

Prophet Zachariah was not rich, but he was always generous, especially to those in need. Now, in a secluded room in the temple there was Mary. She was a pious young girl who lived there alone, far away from the rest of her family. She spent every hour of every day in worship and thanksgiving to God. One day Prophet Zachariah went to check that Mary had everything she needed. From the door of her room he saw a basket of fresh fruit. He was surprised. Besides him, no one else ever came to help her. When he asked how she had gotten the fruit, she told him that the fruit was from God. She found it there every morning. "Why are you so surprised, Uncle," she asked him. "Don't you know that God provides without measure for whomever He wills?"

At ninety years of age Prophet Zachariah had only one regret about his long life. His beloved wife had not been able to have any children. He feared that when he was gone, the people might stray from the right path because they had no one to guide them. They might no longer follow God's laws but they might change the laws to suit themselves. But that day, when he saw Mary's faith in God, he decided to call on God for help. He knew that nothing was impossible for God.

Secretly he prayed, saying, "My Lord! My bones have grown feeble, and my head glistens with gray hair from old age, and, my Lord, I have never been unblessed in my prayer to You. I have fears about how my relatives will behave in continuing my mission, and safeguarding the future of Mary, and my wife is barren. So give me a son who will be my heir in my duty and heir to the straight way of the House of Jacob; and make my son, my Lord, one with whom You are well-pleased."

Then, the angels answered him on God's behalf, "O Zachariah! We give you the good news of a son whose name will be John. We have not given this name to anyone before." He said, "Lord! How will I have a son when my wife is barren and I am already very old and weak?" The angel answered, "It is true. Your Lord says, 'It is easy for Me—I created you before, from nothing.'" Then, Zachariah begged, "My Lord, give me a sign." "Your sign," He said, "is that you will not be able to speak to people for three nights, even though there is nothing wrong with you."

Then, Zachariah came out to his people from the sanctuary and made signs to tell them to glorify God in the morning and in the afternoon. For three days, Prophet Zachariah could not speak out loud, but in his heart he was remembering God and overflowing with love for Him. And after three days he was able to speak again. This is the story of the mercy of God on His servant Zachariah.

PROPHET JOHN (YAHYA)
The Forbearing

عليه السلام

Prophet John was the son God granted to Prophet Zachariah in his old age. John was dutiful and obedient to his parents. As a child he loved to read and study, and God blessed him with piety and wisdom from a very early age.

God guided him to study His law and Prophet John learned all the commandments set down in the Torah. He was the most excellent judge of his people's affairs. He guided people to the right path and warned them against straying. He called on them to repent for their sins. He was always caring and respectful to his elderly parents, as well as to other people.

He liked to sometimes go out of the city into the desert or the mountains to pray and contemplate God's blessings. He never cared about food. He ate what he found there, leaves, herbs, and even locusts. He slept in the mountains or in holes in the ground. Sometimes he would walk into the lair of a mountain lion or a bear as he entered a cave, but because he was concentrating on praising God, he never took fright or even

Prophet John

paid attention to them. The wild animals recognized that John was the Prophet who cared for all creatures, and they would leave their cave empty for him, bowing their heads as they went out. Sometimes he fed the animals out of his own food and fed himself with his prayers. He used to spend the nights crying and praising God for His blessings.

At that time Palestine was ruled by the tyrant king, Herod. The king was planning to marry his beautiful niece, Salome. Out of fear or to gain favors with the ruler, the mother of Salome and some of the men of Israel encouraged Salome to marry the king. On hearing of this plan for marriage, Prophet John handed down a judgment that the marriage was not legal. A man may not marry his niece. It was against the law of the Torah.

His views that this marriage should not occur began to spread around the country, and people began to gossip about the king's unlawful relationship with his niece. Salome was angry, for she was ambitious and wanted to be queen of the kingdom, ruling with her uncle. When King Herod hesitated about their marriage because of Prophet John's ruling, she plotted to get what she wanted. She dressed herself in very attractive clothes so as to tempt him. Then, she went to his throne room and sang and danced before her uncle. Herod wanted her, and he offered her whatever she wished for. She smiled, "I want the head of John because he has defiled your honor and mine throughout the land. If you grant me this wish, I will be yours." Bewitched by her beauty, Herod agreed to the cruel deed. He had Prophet John executed. His compassionate head was presented to cruel Salome on a silver tray. She clapped with delight.

God punished the dreadful murderer of His beloved Prophet. The kingdom of the Israelites was destroyed by invading armies and she and many other sinners like her were tortured and died at the hands of the invaders.

PROPHET JESUS (ISA)
The Healer

One day, while the blessed Mary was worshipping and praising God in the temple, the Spirit sent by God appeared to her in the form of a man. Surprised and fearful, she said, "May God protect me from you, if you do not fear God." The man said, "I am a messenger from your Lord. I am here to announce to you that you will bear a righteous son." Mary was shocked and said, "How can I bear a son when no man has touched me?" The man replied, "If God says to a thing 'Be!', then it is. So, it is easy for Him. And your son will be a sign to humanity and a mercy from God."

The visit by the Spirit caused Mary great worry and anxiety. This increased as the months went by. How could she face the people now that she was to give birth to a child when she had no husband? Later, she felt the baby kicking inside her. With a heavy heart, she left the temple and went to Nazareth, the city in which she had been born. She settled in a simple farmhouse where people would not see her.

After several months, she decided she had to leave Nazareth too, though she was not sure where to go. She had not gone very far when the pains of childbirth started and she could not walk any farther. She sat down and leaned against a dry palm tree. As the pangs of childbirth gripped her and she feared what would happen afterwards, she exclaimed, "I wish I had died before this happened and had vanished into not existing." All alone and out of sight, she gave birth to her son.

As she gazed down at him, suddenly she heard a voice saying, "Do not be sad and anxious your Lord has placed a stream of water at the roots of the tree for you. Shake the trunk of the tree and ripe dates will fall. So eat, drink, get your strength

back, and be happy, for you see the power of God, the One who made the dry palm tree live again in order to provide food for you. If you meet anyone, say, 'I have vowed to fast for God, and may not speak to any human today.'"

As Mary expected, her arrival in the city with a newborn baby disturbed some people. They scolded her, "This is a terrible sin you have committed." Mary put her finger to her lips and pointed to the child. They asked, "How can we speak to a newborn baby?" To their astonishment, the child began to speak aloud, "I am God's servant. God has given me the scripture, the Gospel, and made me a Prophet, and has blessed me wherever I may be, and has enjoined on me prayers and almsgiving as long as I live." Baby Jesus continued, "God has made me dutiful towards she who bore me. Peace be unto me the day I was born, the day I die, and the day I shall be raised alive." Most of the people realized this was a miracle, a sign from God. However, there were others who said that the speech of the baby was a strange magic trick. At least now Mary could stay in Nazareth without problems.

As Jesus grew, the signs of his Prophethood began to increase and grew clearer to everyone around him. Almighty God commanded him to call the children of Israel to the right path. The message of Prophet Jesus was the message of the love of God for others, especially the poor and needy. Prophet Jesus was a living example of all that he said. The people at that time were going away from the original teachings of the Torah revealed to Prophet Moses. Prophet Jesus made it clear that he came not to change the Law but to complete it and reinstate the true teachings of Moses. Those who followed him were the poor and their number was small.

Jesus came into conflict with people who love the things of this world. He told them to stop their hypocrisy, show and false praise. He reminded them of God's great mercy and compassion. He told them that their first duty was to love and worship God, and after that to love their fellow humans. He showed people that the law should allow people to love and help each other.

His teachings infuriated the priests in the temple. He told the people that they could speak to God directly and did not need to pay priests to speak and act on their behalf. He said the law should not be too difficult for

people to obey. But the priests hated this. They were the specialists in law and they earned money from giving advice and judgments.

God aided him by granting him miracles that were also signs of God's mercy and compassion. Prophet Jesus healed the sick by the touch of his hand. He brought people back from the dead. He made a clay bird and then blew on it. It came to life and flew away before people's eyes. He knew people's secrets, what they ate and drank and what they had stored in their houses. When his companions and helpers fasted as he told them, they asked him to request God to send a table from heaven spread with delicious food to break their fast. Prophet Jesus prayed, and their request was granted. When the table was sent down to them, and it was spread with delicious dishes, Prophet Jesus prostrated and thanked God. But only a few years later, his followers forgot that he worshipped the one God in front of them, and they started to worship Prophet Jesus as if he were God.

Prophet Jesus told the people of another Prophet who was going to come after him, whose name would be Prophet Ahmad (meaning Muhammad). He told them the next Prophet would comfort them and would speak only the words God would put into his mouth. There were many people who listened to Prophet Jesus and worshipped God as he taught, but there were some that refused to listen and wanted to destroy him.

The highest council of the Jewish priests met to plot against Jesus. They convinced the Roman governor that Jesus was planning a rebellion against the Roman Empire and urged him to take immediate action against him. The governor ordered that Jesus be arrested. Prophet Jesus was tried and condemned to death. When the evil people were just about to kill Prophet Jesus, God saved him. God caused a criminal to look just like him in their eyes. They took that man and executed him.

The enemies of God boasted, "We killed Jesus!" But they did not kill Prophet Jesus nor did they crucify him. God's miracle caused them to think they had killed him. People who have a different opinion than this are filled with doubt and uncertainty with no real knowledge. The Holy Qur'an says, "For of a surety, they killed him not."

God took Prophet Jesus, body and soul, into the heavens, for God is greater and has power over all of His creatures.

PROPHET MUHAMMAD
The Seal of the Prophets

Prophet Muhammad, peace and blessings be upon him, was born in Mecca, Arabia on the twelfth day of the month of Rabi al-Awwal in 571. His mother's name was Amina. His father was Abdullah, the son of Abdul Muttalib. Prophet Muhammad's family line has been traced back to the noble house of Ishmael, the son of Prophet Abraham to about the fortieth descent. Prophet Muhammad's father died just a few months before he was born, and his mother died when he was six. Then, he was placed first under the care of his grandfather Abdul Muttalib, and then his uncle Abu Talib.

It was the custom at that time for babies born in the city to be kept and suckled for about two years by wet nurses from the desert tribes. A woman named Halima of the tribe known as Bani Saad became Prophet Muhammad's wet nurse.

Prophet Muhammad, peace and blessings be upon him, grew up to be an exceptionally honest man and a successful trader. People called him Al-Amin, the Trustworthy.

At the age of twenty-five, Prophet Muhammad, peace and blessings be upon him, joined a caravan which traveled to Syria on behalf of a noble widow among the Quraysh. Her name was Khadija. He proved so diligent and trustworthy in her business affairs that Khadija sent one of her servants to ask him if he would be interested in marriage. He agreed

and Prophet Muhammad and Khadija married a short time later. Khadija is referred to as the mother of the Muslims. Mother Khadija was older than her husband. She was about forty years old. They had a very happy marriage. Prophet Muhammad, peace and blessings be upon him, said, "The best of the world's women is Khadijah."

The Meccans were descended from Abraham through Ishmael. Their temple, the Ka'ba, had been built by Abraham for the worship of the one God. It was still called the House of God, but now people used it to keep their idols, which they called the "daughters" of God, and other idols. Some Meccans were disgusted by this idol worship, Prophet Muhammad being the first. He wanted to follow the religion of Abraham and tried to find out what he had truly taught.

Prophet Muhammad, peace and blessings be upon him, used to go to a cave in the desert to meditate. The cave was in the Mountain of Light not far from Mecca, and he always went there in Ramadan. One night, towards the end of the month, when he was forty years old, he suddenly heard a voice. It said, "Read!" He said, "I cannot read." The voice said again, "Read!" He said, "I cannot read." An angel took hold of Prophet Muhammad, peace and blessings be upon him, and squeezed the Prophet as much as he could bear, and then a third time the voice, more terrible now, commanded, "Read!" He said, "What shall I read?" The angel once again seized the Prophet and squeezed him and said,

"Read: In the Name of your Lord Who creates.
Creates man from a clot.
Read: And it is your Lord the Most Bountiful
Who teaches by the pen,
Teaches man that which he knew not."

He went out of the cave onto the hillside and heard the voice say, "O Muhammad! You are God's messenger, and I am Gabriel." He looked up and saw the angel in the sky above the horizon. And again the same voice said,

"O Muhammad! You are God's messenger, and I am Gabriel." Prophet Muhammad's mission as a messenger started with this extraordinary event.

Khadija, the wife of God's Messenger, was the first in her time to become a believer and to follow Prophet Muhammad in prayer to Almighty God. Prophet Muhammad's cousin, Ali, was the next to believe and become a Companion of the Prophet. The third was his servant Zayd, a former slave, and Prophet Muhammad's old friend Abu Bakr was also among the first believers. For three years he preached to his family and friends, but only thirty people became believers.

Then, God told Prophet Muhammad, peace and blessings be upon him, to begin approaching the people of Mecca. He chose beautiful words to tell them of the wishes of God, hoping this would appeal to them. Prophet Muhammad told them that there is no god but God, and that they must worship Him only. He said that they should share their food and clothes with the poor, the sick must be nursed and the orphans must be cared for.

Most of the Meccans just laughed at what Prophet Muhammad, peace and blessings be upon him, told them. Still worse, they refused to worship God and continued believing that it was more important to have a lot of money and worship idols. But when he began to criticize their idols, they grew angry. They insulted him. They threw stones and filth at him when he was praying. During these hard times, his uncle Abu Talib was protecting him. Things got worse and worse. They even killed some of those who followed him and believed in one God. The Muslims in the first four years were mostly poor people who had no powerful friends to defend them. So cruelly were they treated that the Prophet advised all who could do so to flee to a nearby Christian country, Abyssinia. Many of them left Mecca for several years and lived as refugees in Abyssinia.

Still the number of Muslims in Mecca increased. The Quraysh's hatred grew, and finally Abu Talib could not defend the small group anymore. The people of Mecca drove Muhammad, his family, his relatives, and his friends out of the town.

Prophet Muhammad

The Muslims made camp in a valley in the mountains outside Mecca. They were forced to stay in that bare and unsheltered place in the desert for almost three years. They had no food and the Meccans would not help them. Prophet Muhammad's beloved wife died there. Her health failed because of the hard conditions. After three long years, they were allowed to go about the city again.

Prophet Muhammad, peace and blessings be upon him, still had no success preaching to the Meccans. Then, in the pilgrimage season, he met a group of men from Yathrib who were pleased to hear what he said. Prophet Muhammad was inspired to move his people to Yathrib, which is now called Medina. The Muslims' emigration from Mecca marks the beginning of the Islamic calendar. The Prophet sent all the other believers before him, so he and his friend Abu Bakr were almost the last ones to leave Mecca. But driving Prophet Muhammad, peace and blessings be upon him, and his followers out of town was not enough for the disbelievers. When they saw he had not given up and that more people were starting to believe him, once again they decided to kill him. Prophet Muhammad saw the men lurking outside his house waiting to kill him as he left. He asked his cousin Ali to lie in his bed under a blanket so that if the Meccans looked in, they would think that the Prophet was still there. He let Ali know that he would see him later. Then, the Prophet walked out of his house right under the gang's noses. God hid the Prophet from the assassins and they did not see him and Abu Bakr pass by.

The gang waited all night. They peeked through the window and saw someone lying in the bed. In the morning, Ali came out. When those evil people realized that it was Ali who had been in Prophet Muhammad's bed and that the Prophet had left a long time earlier, they became very angry.

Prophet Muhammad and Abu Bakr avoided the road from Mecca to Medina, where they could be seen by the assassins. They wanted to avoid being followed and caught. They went on foot, climbing the rocky slopes to the caves near Mecca.

By nightfall they had reached the caves, but they could hear the hooves of their enemies' horses getting closer. "What shall we do," said Abu Bakr, "when there are only two of us?" Prophet Muhammad, peace and blessings be upon him, led him into a cave. "No," he said, "God is with us."

Footsteps approached the mouth of the cave. Abu Bakr could hardly breathe. Then, they heard, "They aren't here. It's covered with a spider's web and there's a nest. No one has been here for years." They heard the footsteps moving away, and the horses' hooves riding into the distance. Abu Bakr praised God and opened his eyes. The cave entrance was different. Stretched across it they saw a beautiful, silver spider's web, and in front of it, outside the cave, there was a low branch with a nest where a dove sat, cooing gently. "How did that happen?" wondered Abu Bakr. The Prophet simply smiled. When they were certain the enemy had gone, they left the cave that had protected them, and continued their journey safely to Medina. This journey that Prophet Muhammad, peace and blessings be upon him, made is known as the Hijra, and the Islamic calendar starts from the year of Hijra which is 622 CE.

In Medina, Prophet Muhammad, peace and blessings be upon him, and the believers built a mosque. Here they prayed five times every day. Prophet Muhammad continued to receive the messages of God from the Angel Gabriel. These messages were revealed to Prophet Muhammad, then his followers and friends memorized them and wrote them down on leaves and tree bark. These revelations are called the Holy Qur'an.

Besides the Holy Qur'an, Prophet Muhammad was blessed with many miracles. On one occasion in Mecca, he pointed to the moon, and the moon split into two at God's command. When Muslims were in need of water, he prayed to God and water started to pour from his hands. With God's grace on him, Prophet Muhammad showed hundreds of miracles to his community to prove that he was the messenger of God.

Prophet Muhammad, peace and blessings be upon him, and his followers had to defend themselves against the attacks of the disbelievers. There were many battles between them. After long years of warfare both sides agreed to sign a peace treaty at Hudaybiya.

Although some of the Muslims felt that the treaty was not fair, over the next year the wisdom of the treaty became clearer and clearer. More and more people from the unbelieving tribes came to Islam. Meccans too began to become Muslims. Finally, in the following year, the eighth year of Hijra, they were able to return to Mecca for the pilgrimage. The previous year, there had been only three hundred of them, but now they came in great numbers. God had helped the Muslims as He had promised; the chiefs of the unbelievers, who had withdrawn to the hills to watch from afar, were shocked and dismayed to see how the number of Muslims had grown. After this, many of the Muslims moved back to live in Mecca and the number of Meccans embracing Islam also continued to grow.

In the tenth year of Hijra many thousands of people entered Islam. Envoys came from many lands, even as far as China, to find out about this religion. In that year God's Messenger performed the pilgrimage with a multitude of forty thousand. However, this pilgrimage was also filled with sorrow because the Holy Prophet warned the people, "It may be that you will not see me among you in this place after this year."

During this pilgrimage, he gave several sermons to the believers. He declared that the days of blood feuds between the tribes were over and that the Muslims must forgive each other past wrongs and cease fighting against and killing each other. He reminded them to be trustworthy and always keep their word in their business dealings and anything to do with money or property. He ordered them never to charge or pay interest on loans and declared any interest payments owed at that time to be waived. He reminded them that God had set the laws of inheritance, and they should be faithful to those laws. He ordered them to be just in dealing with crime and criminals and to recall that forgiveness is better than revenge. He warned men and women to be fair to each other and that husbands have rights over their wives, just as their wives have rights over them. He commanded men to take care of women and provide for them. He reminded them that all humans come from Adam and Adam was made of clay. So all humans are equal and nobody can be superior to anyone else because of his or her tribe or nation, but only by his or her good deeds and piety. All believers are brothers and sisters, and they should not go against each other's rights. He told them that he was leaving behind him the Qur'an and that if they held tight to it, they would never go astray. "Be my witness, O God" concluded the Holy Prophet, "that I have conveyed Your message to Your people."

Shortly after his return from the pilgrimage, the Holy Prophet fell ill with a fever. One night, as his fever grew worse, he became too ill to lead the community in prayer in the mosque so he appointed Abu Bakr to lead the congregation in the night prayer. As Abu Bakr led the prayer, he began to weep. The next morning, the Messenger of God was helped to the mosque and he followed Abu Bakr in the prayer from a seated position. Then, he prayed for the community and for all of the Prophets and he instructed the people to cling to the faith. Next, he asked, "Have you heard of the Lord's servant who was asked by Him, 'What do you love more, this world or the world to come?' The man chose the world to come. His Lord was pleased with his servant and promised to admit him to his Lord's presence." Abu Bakr began to weep at this, understanding that the Prophet was soon to pass from this world. The Prophet consoled him, "Abu Bakr, you will be with me in the other world," and turning to the people he said, "Nobody has shown me such friendship as he." He reminded the congregation of the Day of Judgment and asked their forgiveness if any of them felt he had wronged them, and he forgave anybody who had wronged him. Then he left the mosque and went to lie in the room of his wife Aisha.

On Friday, after three more days, his illness had become very severe. He looked at his Companions, who had gathered around him, and reminded them again of their duties to God and each other. He prayed for them and encouraged them, and then he sank back onto a cushion. A few days later, the Messenger of God recovered for a short while and all the Companions were relieved. But suddenly, his death agony came upon him and he passed away in the arms of his wife Aisha. Ali stepped out of the room weeping but Umar told him to stop. "He has not died. He has just gone to the presence of his Lord and he will come back," said Umar. "If anyone says he is dead, I will cut off their head!" Then, Abu Bakr came and pulled back the cloak over the Prophet's face and kissed him before covering him again. "Umar, do not speak like that" he said, "for in the Qur'an God says to our Prophet, 'You are mortal and they are mortal.'"

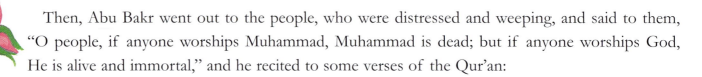

Prophet Muhammad

Then, Abu Bakr went out to the people, who were distressed and weeping, and said to them, "O people, if anyone worships Muhammad, Muhammad is dead; but if anyone worships God, He is alive and immortal," and he recited to some verses of the Qur'an:

"Muhammad is but a Messenger, and Messengers passed away before him. If, then, he dies or is killed, will you turn back on your heels? Whoever turns back on his heels can in no way harm God. But God will reward the thankful ones. It never occurs that a soul dies except by God's will, at a time appointed. So whoever desires the reward of this world, We give him of it; and whoever desires the reward of the Hereafter, We give him of it; and We will soon reward the thankful."

Today Muslims travel to Mecca on pilgrimage or hajj. The Ka'ba, which Prophet Ishmael and Prophet Abraham built together, still stands in Mecca. When we bow down and prostrate in the direction of the Ka'ba five times a day in our prayers, it reminds us that there is nothing like God, and nothing else is worthy of worship except God. Muslims believe in God as the only being worthy of worship and strive to please Him by worship and by doing good deeds.